Great Olympic Moments

Steve Redgrave

headline

To Mom and Dad for being such great parents throughout my life

Contents

Introduction

As a ten-year old boy, I was inspired to begin my own sporting journey after watching the legendary swimmer Mark Spitz win a record-breaking haul of gold medals at the Munich Olympics in 1972. Little did I know that, twenty-eight years later, I would be entering the record books myself after winning my fifth gold medal at the Sydney Olympics in 2000. The Olympic games have been absolutely central to my career and my life, which is why I have chosen to share with you my selection of *Great Olympic Moments* in this book.

For me, each Olympics I have competed in has conjured up a fascinating mixture of sensations, from the gut-wrenching physical pain of intense competition to the elation of winning and the knowledge that I have given absolutely everything in pursuit of a dream. The Olympic dream was sparked into motion by visionary French aristocrat Pierre Coubertin, who believed that the well-being of entire nations could be enhanced by striving to achieve sporting excellence. Indeed, the realisation of that dream with the staging of the first modern Olympics in Athens in 1896 could also be regarded as a great moment in itself.

Some of the moments I have chosen to include, such as the Munich hostage crisis of 1972, are tragic rather than celebratory. I have also included episodes which deal with the competitive misfortune of individual athletes as well as the stories of those who have sought to gain an unfair advantage by cheating. Such is sport and life. The story of the Olympics is one of both elation and dejection, success and ignominy, and it would be remiss not to include moments that reflect this, however painful some of those memories are.

In Brazil in 2016, golf will re-enter the Olympic family of events, and rugby (sevens format) is also included for the very first time. I have chosen to recount my golfing experience with Tiger Woods in Hyde Park shortly after the Sydney Olympics in 2000, to demonstrate what the Olympics means to all, even one of the greatest sportsmen on the planet. I hope that the newly-included sports will deliver their core integrity to the Olympics in the same way that many other sports and individual athletes have done before them. Whilst this is a book focussed mainly on the summer Olympics, I have also included a selection of moments from the winter games. The inclusion of Ingemar Stenmark's double gold at Lake Placid in 1980 is an homage to the sport of skiing which is a personal passion of mine.

I fully acknowledge that you will have your own personal recollection of the Olympics. My selection is by no means definitive and won't necessarily match your own. What I hope it will do is bring vividly to life the true wonder of the Olympics, and reveal some of the more unlikely and less-well known events in Olympic history. If nothing else, this book should help you ignite some healthy debate among your friends and family.

To my mind, the Olympics are a truly unique event, where individuals and nations come together, united in a kindred spirit of healthy, glorious competition. To those that have competed in the past, I raise my thanks. They have inspired me and countless others throughout the years and will continue to do so. I am extremely proud that the Olympics are returning to Great Britain in 2012, and to those athletes yet to compete, I look forward to witnessing those, who, by their actions, will make the Olympic flame glow even brighter.

Ben Ainslie
Sydney 2000
Laser Fleet Sailing

I wouldn't call anyone in sport – or life, for that matter – a kindred spirit, but Britain's greatest sailor, Ben Ainslie, comes closer than most. I, too, messed around in boats for years, I won gold medals at successive Olympic Games and for a huge length of time no one took much notice.

At Los Angeles in 1984, my debut Olympics, you couldn't exactly say that the BBC built up to the coxed fours with a fanfare. 'Right,' said Des Lynam, the BBC anchorman, from behind his desk, 'and now we go over to Lake Casitas where we have a chance of a medal.' Zoom into start line. There we were.

I could never really understand why the *fifth* gold medal warranted documentaries and a knighthood and a BBC Sports Personality of the Year award, while the fourth, the third, the second and the first did not. Perhaps that is just me being pedantic, but they were the same achievement each time.

Perhaps this is when it will kick on for Ainslie. London 2012 is set to be his fifth Olympics. He began his medal chase in Atlanta with silver in the Laser class, followed by golds at the next three Olympics, which included an incredible weight gain of 15kg (33lb) to take part in the bigger, heavier Finn class.

I, too, messed around in boats for years, I won gold medals at successive Olympic Games and for a huge length of time no one took much notice.

What a joy that must be – licence to eat cake. Sadly, my weight gains have all been illicit.

Yet Ben has emerged from all these great performances without the recognition I think he deserves. Unlike his fellow sailors, Sir Walter Raleigh, Sir Francis Drake, Dame Ellen MacArthur, he has yet to feel the touch of the Queen's sword on his shoulder and I'm mystified as to why that should be.

Put it this way, Kelly Holmes won two golds in one Olympics and was rewarded with the status of a Dame. Nothing should be taken away from her tremendous performance and recognition, but Ben has, to date, won a silver and three golds in four successive Olympics and has so far worked his way up to a CBE. Why? If comparing, I would suggest his performance is the superior of the two. Is his achievement really less valuable?

I put it down to politics. I can't help being cynical and concluding that the honours system is entirely about the desire of politicians to cosy up to people in the heavy media limelight. Men in boats aren't as immediately attractive and triumphant as a double gold-medal-winning track athlete on the front pages of every newspaper – especially when, as in Ben's case, so much of his sport takes place far out to sea, and you seem to be watching a watery dot most of the time. It doesn't help that

I can't help being cynical and concluding that the honours system is entirely about the desire of politicians to cosy up to people in the heavy media limelight. Men in boats aren't as immediately attractive and triumphant as a double gold-medal-winning track athlete on the front pages of every newspaper.

So much of his sport takes place far out to sea, and you seem to be watching a watery dot most of the time. It doesn't help that the nature of the action is often unclear, involving convoluted calculations of time, tide and wind, and sometimes the boats just seem to sit on the spot.

the nature of the action is often unclear, involving convoluted calculations of time, tide and wind, and sometimes the boats just seem to sit on the spot.

This was very true in Sydney in 2000 when Ben's gold medal was dependent upon beating the Brazilian, Robert Scheidt, in the final race of the series. Ben simply needed to stay ahead of his rival to win gold, so instead of racing in the conventional sense, he took an immediate lead and then seemed to hang about. In fact, connoisseurs acknowledged that he was behaving with great tactical astuteness, preventing his opponent getting past him. To the rest of us, it just looked like floating.

Ben has gone on to have a glittering career – more Olympic gold medals, three times World Sailor of the Year, appointed captain of the GB America's Cup team before they pulled out of the 2013 event – and yet the knighthood is still pending.

Bob Beamon

Mexico 1968
Long jump final

This is an extraordinary picture. It looks like the athlete is being catapulted, literally, to Olympic stardom. He's so high off the ground and looks so shocked, it's almost as though he can hardly believe it himself.

This is a rare moment, the thin air of Mexico City creating a picture, a feat, a legend, that Beamon himself would never be able to recreate – one of those elusive split seconds when it all comes together, the almost-impossible dream. In this case, his run-up (he was a sprinter by trade) was fantastically fast, the take-off perfect to a millimetre, the height prodigious and the flight just seemed to go on forever. When he eventually came back to earth, it was as the record-breaking Olympic champion.

If only one of the lady judges hadn't missed it. Where can she have been looking? At least her colleague, in the smart hat, is leaning forward, apparently stunned, probably thinking, 'Can I believe what I'm seeing?'

What she was seeing was the flight of a human cannonball. Put it this way. The world record, jointly held by Ralph Boston of the USA and Igor Ter-Ovanesyan of the Soviet Union, was 27ft 4¾in. Bob Beamon sailed through that. He approached the 28ft barrier and sailed through that, too. He kept on sailing. He approached the 29ft barrier and he sailed through that. He finally came to rest, with a thud, at a distance of 29ft 2½in. He landed with such force that he bounced out of the pit altogether.

The stunned snatches of conversation that subsequently took place have been handed down through posterity.

'That's over 28 feet!' gasped record-holder Boston to reigning Olympic champion, Lynn Davies of Wales.

'With his first jump? No, it can't be.'

> '*That's over 28 feet!*'
> Ralph Boston

> '*With his first jump? No, it can't be.*'
> Lynn Davies

Meanwhile, the officials had gone to search out an old-fashioned steel tape measure because the leap had surpassed their electronic marker's capabilities. Eventually, after a long pause, '8.90m' flashed up on the scoreboard. Beamon, unfamiliar with the metric system, had no idea what it meant. Boston had to explain it to him. 'Bob, you jumped 29 feet.'

So overwhelmed was Beamon that his legs gave way and he sank to the floor in what doctors later described as a 'cataleptic seizure' brought on by emotional shock. His Soviet rival was pretty shocked, too.

'Compared to this jump, we are as children,' said Ter-Ovanesyan.

Davies put it even more starkly. 'I can't go on,' he said. He barely did. He finished ninth.

Some legendary sporting moments are a matter of culmination – Michael Johnson in Atlanta, for example, or Ingemar Stenmark at Lake Placid. Others are more freakish. Beamon's jump was king of the freaks, but not because Bob Beamon was not a tremendous athlete. He was. The 6ft 3in 22-year-old from South Jamaica, New York, had won 22 of his last 23 meetings. But, somewhat hit-or-miss down the runway, he was prone to foul jumping. He had also been without a coach for the four months leading up to the Olympics because he was suspended for refusing to compete against Brigham Young University as a protest against racial Mormon policies.

So overwhelmed was Beamon that his legs gave way and he sank to the floor in what doctors later described as a 'cataleptic seizure' brought on by emotional shock.

After this monumental moment in his life, Beamon never jumped farther than 26ft 11½in.

So he was not the unarguable favourite for the event. It is not even certain he would have survived the qualifying rounds, had not his generous fellow-countryman, Boston, given him a hint about how to handle his errant jumping just before his last-chance leap to qualify. I wonder if Boston ever regretted it.

Having qualified, just, Beamon then awaited his first jump in the competition final. He wasn't even confident himself. In fact, he was fretting about the fact that he'd had sex the night before. Beamon found himself worrying about the fact that he might have expended vital energy the night before his big event. The evidence would suggest not.

At the time, Beamon's jump was hailed as the greatest athletic achievement of all time, and it has to be right up there. Look at the figures. Since Jesse Owens' record-breaking jump of 26ft 8¼in in 1935, the world record had progressed 8½in in 33 years. In seconds, Beamon had added another 21¾in. Nearly two feet! It is almost incredible.

So I don't apologise for the word 'freak' to describe Beamon's colossal jump in Mexico. And this is my final evidence. After this monumental moment in his life, Beamon never jumped farther than 26ft 11½in.

Fanny Blankers-Koen

London 1948
Athletics

A London Olympics soaked by torrential rain. Fancy that! But what this photo really tells me is that women's athletics has changed beyond recognition in half a century.

I exonerate Fanny Blankers-Koen, the Dutch 'Flying Housewife' who left the rest of the field for dead in this sprint, but look at the rest of them. They scarcely seemed to have muscles in those days and they bear absolutely no resemblance to the modern female athlete. Post-war and pre-intensive professional training, perhaps that is understandable, but it makes you realise how far sportswomen, in particular, have come.

In my own sport, rowing, women were not allowed to compete in the Olympics until 1976, and even then they were limited to a distance of 1000 metres. For most of the century, women were barred from almost all endurance sports, because it was feared that the delicacy of their condition (i.e. being female) would cause them to collapse or, worse, appear unladylike. Baron de Coubertin, founder of the modern Olympics, would certainly not have foreseen female weightlifters.

Londoners were frankly incredulous that a woman from Holland, 30 years old and married with two children, aged seven and two, should think of competing in five Olympic events.

Although she arrived in London as the holder of seven world records, the scepticism surrounding her was almost total. A mother, aged 30! She was practically disqualified on those grounds alone.

I am saying all this, confident that I am on the right side of the argument. I was brought up in a household that included strong, practical women. My mum ran two local clubs. When my sister moved into her new home and found she could see the sky through a broken roof, she rolled up her sleeves and fixed it herself. I remember one time when my dad had somehow acquired a lorry-load of ready-mix cement for our drive. It arrived around teatime and all of us had to go out – Mum, Dad, my sisters and me – to lay it down before it dried. There was no question of anyone pulling some 'I'm just a weak woman' line. We all got on with it. Now I live in another household where women are in the majority. My son and the dog redress the balance slightly, but sexist attitudes would not be tolerated.

That was not the case at the Austerity Games in 1948. Londoners were frankly incredulous that a woman from Holland, 30 years old and married with two children, aged seven and two, should think of competing in five Olympic events. It was neither seemly nor possible in their eyes. And so Fanny Blankers-Koen not only staggered her audience by galloping to four gold medals – she withdrew from the long jump to concentrate on the hurdles – but she may even have rewired the cultural assumptions of the time.

She was a farmer's daughter whose proudest Olympic moment prior to London was getting Jesse Owens' autograph at the Berlin Games in 1936 at the age of 18. The Second World War deprived her of any further Olympic opportunity, and although she arrived in London as the holder of seven world records, the scepticism surrounding her was almost total. A mother, aged 30! She was practically disqualified on those grounds alone.

Perhaps this was the point in British history when male attitudes had to shift. Women had been fighting a world war, and now they were producing heroic performances on the global sporting stage.

The critics were soon in retreat. She won the 100 yards (as it was then) by three full yards in the rain, and later in the week she went on to victory in the 80 metres hurdles, the 200 metres and the 4 x 400 metres relay, in which, on the anchor leg, she overtook runners for Britain, Canada and Australia to claim the victory for Holland. Of the nine women's track and field events included in the London programme, she had won four and would probably have won five if her coach/husband hadn't talked her out of the long jump for fear it would blight her chances in the hurdles. So it was all a man's fault that her achievement was not even more ground-breaking.

Perhaps this was the point in British history when male attitudes had to shift. Women had been fighting a world war, and now they were producing heroic performances on the global sporting stage. They could hardly be consigned to kitchen and cleaning duties any more, much though antediluvian men would enjoy it. Myself, I am a great contributor to household chores, I can cook my kids spaghetti bolognese and I accept there are certain jobs that males simply have to do, such as buying the TV licence – also watching TV, otherwise it's a waste. As for dusting, what's that?

Chris Boardman

Barcelona 1992
4000 metre individual pursuit final

I like Chris a lot. We've met quite a few times at Olympic Games, both old blokes in the commentary box. In Barcelona, we were two of eight Britons to win gold medals,* but funnily enough, I didn't see him there at all. We were locked in our own sporting bubbles, I suppose. But I remember being impressed by his Lotus Superbike, which was visibly different from its predecessors, with a solid back wheel and carbon-fibre frame. The bike and the swept-back helmet signalled the dawning of the space age in cycle racing. He absolutely trounced his opponent in the final of the 4000 metre individual pursuit in the Barcelona Velodrome, actually lapping him, which is rare in a time trial.

Years later, he admitted the level of his commitment, his obsession. I remember him saying that the morning after his wedding he was up incredibly early to check out a course he'd be racing on later. He didn't even think about it. That was his

---

* The other Olympic medal-winners from Barcelona are (because I enjoy knowing such bloke-list things): Linford Christie, Sally Gunnell, Matt Pinsent, Johnny Searle, Greg Searle and – this will have taken you some brain teasing – Garry Herbert, the cox in the Searle brothers pair.

I think I had an unhealthy attitude, too, although slightly less pronounced. It can happen all too easily in the world of élite sport.

priority. He missed the birth of at least one of his children for the same reason. This is what he said about it.

'At the time I was so wrapped up in my career that I felt a bit bad about this, but that was it. I treated it as an occupational hazard. It's only when I look back that I realise how frightening were the extremes I would go to and how focused I was. It certainly wasn't rational or healthy, but it was what separated me from the crowd really – [the ability] to apply myself to an unreasonable degree. I would forget things like birthdays because I was just completely wrapped up in other things. Even if I was physically there, my mind would be thinking about how whatever I was doing would impact on training and performance.'

He's right. I think it was probably unhealthy. I think I had an unhealthy attitude, too, although slightly less pronounced. It can happen all too easily in the world of élite sport. Training and performance can become your priority, over and above the other connections in your life. To be the best you can be ultimately means a sacrifice somewhere down the line. That sacrifice is often other people. Am I trying to say I was a selfish so-and-so? Probably. Am I sorry? Probably not.

'I would forget things like birthdays because I was just completely wrapped up in other things. Even if I was physically there, my mind would be thinking about how whatever I was doing would impact on training and performance.'

Chris Boardman

To be the best you can be ultimately means a sacrifice somewhere down the line. That sacrifice is often other people. Am I trying to say I was a selfish so-and-so? Probably. Am I sorry? Probably not.

Luckily, I was married to Ann, who had herself rowed at the highest level. She'd competed in the Olympic Games in 1984, and so she knew and understood what it took to be successful. It was no surprise to her that I had to commit a huge amount of time and energy to rowing, leaving her, a doctor with a practice of her own, to do everything else.

To be absolutely fair, our first daughter wasn't planned. I didn't know what to think when Ann first told me. I didn't think we'd ever talked about having babies, although we both knew we wanted a family at some point. But pretty soon I realised I was very pleased.

Even so, like Chris Boardman, I wasn't planning on being at the birth. The date clashed with one of our training camps in Austria – this was 1991, prior to the Olympics in Barcelona – and so I was expecting to be halfway up a mountain when Ann went into labour. Ann wasn't unhappy about this. She understood, as she did so many times. Her biggest stress was whether or not one of my rowing pals, Roger, really meant it when he said he'd video the birth for me to watch later.

In the event, the planning didn't matter. Natalie arrived three-and-a-half weeks early and I was there at the birth, being a heroic help, I'm sure. I was there for the arrival of my other two children, too, and we still seem to have a functional family, so no harm done.

Steve Bradbury

Salt Lake City 2002
1000 metres speed skating

Sometimes, let's face it, you just get lucky. I have been. Supposing my old school teacher, Francis Smith, hadn't loved rowing and hadn't bothered to take a cluster of boisterous boys down to the river every night. Where would I have spent my life? On a construction site is my best guess, with an unhealthy love of biscuits and beer.

But this guy, he really won the jackpot. What I like about the story of Australian speed skater Steve Bradbury is that he never even had a glimmer of expectation going into the competition from which he would emerge with a gold medal. He was older, slower, flat out worse than the other competitors. He only made the final because one of the skaters who got through in the semis was disqualified, and his tactics going into the Olympic final were, essentially, stay out of trouble at the back.

As you see, there was quite a bit of trouble to be had. Revving it up round the final bend caused a pile-up between all four of his rivals, and the Aussie skated to the line, bewildered,

He only made the final because one of the skaters who got through in the semis was disqualified, and his tactics going into the Olympic final were, essentially, stay out of trouble at the back.

Ohno, apart from having the most perfect name for the headline writers in the circumstances, remains the most decorated US Winter Olympic athlete of all time. But not that day.

stunned and elated, to claim the Southern Hemisphere's first ever gold in Winter Olympic history.

Can you imagine how Mathieu Turcott of Canada felt about that – the skater in the picture with his head rammed against the boards and his helmet skewed over his eyes; or Hyun-Soo Ahn of South Korea, on his backside with his legs in the air; or, and especially, Apolo Anton Ohno of America, about to struggle to his feet and claim the silver? Ohno, apart from having the most perfect name for the headline writers in the circumstances, remains the most decorated US Winter Olympic athlete of all time. But not that day.

I also think that the speed-skating sprint is not really a sport. It's an exhibition, an entertainment. It is a crash waiting to happen.

I was in Salt Lake City and I seem to remember the US media being rather sniffy about the winner. The newspaper *USA Today* said Bradbury's gold medal 'fell out of the sky like a bagged goose. He looked like a tortoise behind four hares.' But his fellow Australians gave him a homecoming to remember. They made him a folk hero, created a 45c stamp with his face on it and even inducted his name into the language. Forever, 'doing a Bradbury' meant achieving something way, way beyond all natural expectations.

My reaction is somewhere in the middle of the two. I think it's funny, but I also think that the speed-skating sprint is not really a sport. It's an exhibition, an entertainment. It is a crash waiting to happen. It adds a different dimension to the Olympics and I wouldn't necessarily like to see it thrown out, but I'm aware that it is not a purist sport.

To my mind, it's a little bit like snowboarding cross or 20-20 cricket – a spectacular version of the traditional sport – and because of its brevity, risks are taken and accidents happen. It's car-crash sport, and on this occasion, I have to admit it made me laugh.

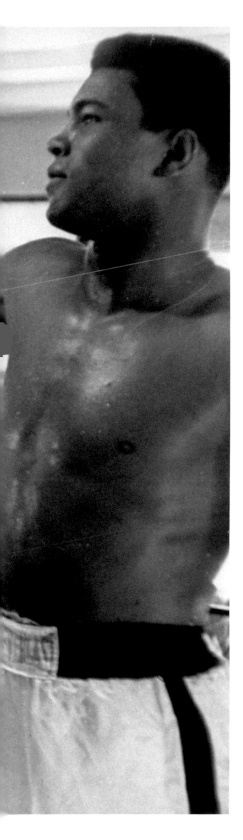

Cassius Clay
Rome 1960
Light-heavyweight boxing

He had everything, didn't he? He was everything a sportsman would like to be – talented, charismatic, had the gift-of-the-gab, a winner. I loved boxing when I was a kid. I wanted to be like him. I had my own little punchbag on a wooden base that you stood on to stop it falling over when you hit it. But it was pretty evident that despite my long reach and going-on-heavyweight build, I was more cut out for the river than the ring.

I knew Ali, of course, from his famous fights against Frazier and Foreman, and his interviews – plus poems – with Michael Parkinson on the BBC. I didn't really know much about his one appearance at the Olympics, but the story he told about it – perhaps a little theatrically exaggerated, knowing Ali – bears retelling.

He was an 18-year-old kid from Louisville, Kentucky, Cassius Marcellus Clay, when he travelled to Rome for the Olympics to compete in the *light*-heavyweight – not the heavyweight – competition. Needless to say, he loved the atmosphere in the village, introduced himself to everyone, chatted, took photos, was the life and soul of the athletic party. (The absolute and utter reverse of me at an Olympics, by the way.) Despite his youth, he cruised to the final where he met Zbigniew Pietrzykowski, from Poland, three-time European champion and veteran of 231 fights. Clay won by unanimous decision. He had his gold medal.

At the press conference afterwards he was asked by a Russian journalist how he felt about not being allowed, as a Negro, to eat in certain restaurants in America. Fiercely patriotic and inexperienced, Clay retorted, typically, 'Russian, we got qualified men working on that problem. We got the biggest and the prettiest cars. We got all the food we can eat. America is the greatest country in the world, and as far as places I can't eat goes, I got lots of places I can eat – more places I can than I can't.'

I look at that answer in awe. Had I gone to the Moscow Olympics as an 18-year-old, I think the most the local journalists would have got out of me was a grunt. Even four years later, after Los Angeles, I was almost completely tongue-tied when the mayor of Marlow wanted me to say a few words. Maybe it's one of the reasons I always admired Ali so much.

At least we had this in common – he appreciated his gold medal. In fact, he loved it. Slept with it, ate with it, wore it all the time. The gold leaf began to wear off, he spent so much time in its company. By now, he had turned professional and gradually regretted his response to the Soviet journalist. His youthful enthusiasm for all things American had faded like the red, white and blue paint his dad had daubed on the front-porch steps of their home when his teenaged son returned, a hero, from Rome.

The story of his disillusion, as Ali told it later, is that he and a friend in Louisville stopped one day at a whites-only restaurant and tried to order two burgers and two vanilla milkshakes. They were refused service. Clay played his trump card. 'Miss,' he said to the waitress, 'I'm Cassius Clay, the Olympic champion,' showing off to her his by now slightly battered gold medal. The owner of the restaurant interrupted and called to the waitress, 'I don't give a damn who he is! I done told you, we don't serve no niggers!'

In Ali's words, everything changed in that moment. 'Whatever illusions I'd built up in Rome as the all-American boy were gone. My Olympic honeymoon was over.' There was a fight, supposedly, with a white gang and then he walked to the middle of a bridge over the Ohio River and threw his medal into the water. 'I saw it as it was. Ordinary. Just an object.'

It's a compelling picture. All the more vivid to me since my medals have continued to mean so much in my life. But

I completely respect his feelings, given the civil rights issues at the time in America. Many people have doubted the story about him throwing the medal away. It may have sounded a little too neat and symbolic to be likely. Either way, the medal was never seen again.

But the wheel turns and I remember being in the Olympic Stadium in Atlanta over 30 years later for the opening ceremony, where I was the British flag-bearer. Matt and I were always intrigued to guess who was going to light the Olympic flame – and this time we had no idea. The President? Carl Lewis? Some baseball star we'd never heard of? It never occured to me that my ultimate sporting hero would be the man.

I was genuinely surprised, and in a way saddened, when I saw this figure, all in white, standing, visibly shaking from the symptoms of his illness, ready to light the flame. But in another way, I thought how fitting that the greatest athlete of the 20th century should have his place again in Olympic history. It was a moving moment and I, who would avoid ceremonies of most kinds if I could, was grateful for once to be there. He remains, Ali, despite the controversies and his sad decline into illness, 'The Greatest' athlete and character I've ever seen.

Ironically, I've been close to him twice but never managed to speak to him. I sat one seat away from him at the BBC Sports Personality of the Year, but given that the obstacle between us was man-mountain and former heavyweight champion Lennox Lewis, I didn't have the opportunity to say hello. I was also a guest at his 60th birthday party in London – we sat on the next table – but he wouldn't have known who I was and I'm too reserved to go up to anyone myself. I will always admire him from afar.

There is a strange rider to this story, which explains why I have included the picture of Ali and the Beatles. Partly it just demonstrates the height of Ali's fame – those great talents of the 20th century playing about together – but it also reminds me of my fleeting friendship with George Harrison, whom I came to know quite by chance just before my fifth Olympics.

He walked to the middle of a bridge over the Ohio River and threw his medal into the water. 'I saw it as it was. Ordinary. Just an object.'

You might think I haven't much in common with cultural icons from the rock world, and you would be right. It wasn't me who formed the connection but my wife, Ann. She occasionally went to George's house in Henley in her capacity as an osteopath, to treat both George and Olivia, his wife. We both knew their son, Danny, who came to the Leander Club from time to time because he'd coxed a couple of crews at university. They lived locally to us, Henley to our Marlow, so I knew them without really knowing them, if you see what I mean.

One particular day, just before the last World Cup race in Lucerne – and most significantly, our last race before the Sydney Olympics – Ann had been to their house to treat them and as she was leaving, Olivia called up to George, 'Ann's going now. Don't forget to wish Steve luck for Lucerne.' He called back, 'Oh, he doesn't need my luck. They'll win no problem.'

Well, we lost, and George, a great believer in karma, was absolutely devastated. He thought it was all his fault. So not long before Sydney, he and Olivia invited us round for tea so that I could meet him for the first time and he could right the wrong. The thing I remember most is that he was such a nice guy – no star-like behaviour, or anything to suggest so-called celebrity. He was just a really decent, almost ordinary man – if you can say such a thing about a Beatle. I ended up feeling quite sorry for him because his fame had given him an image so far removed from reality.

We had a lovely, normal time and when we were leaving, he rushed off and came back with a little wooden Buddha – this time to wish me luck properly. You can probably guess how much I believe in other-worldly influences (not much!) but I admit that little figure came with me to Sydney. And we won. I can't really imagine that it was entirely down to George's good karma, but on the other hand, the Buddha came back in our luggage and it remains here somewhere.

I was genuinely surprised, and in a way saddened, when I saw this figure, all in white, standing, visibly shaking from the symptoms of his illness, ready to light the flame.

Seb Coe
Moscow 1980
1500 metres final

You are looking at a human being in the process of an exorcism. This is nothing less than the crucial moment of redemption that allowed Seb Coe to pick up the thread of his athletic life after a globally publicised and traumatic failure.

Back in 1980, you were either a Coe or an Ovett person. Their rivalry as British middle-distance runners was real, intense and polarising. I was an Ovett man, because he was a bit of a rebel, like I am, and he often used to compete in a red vest, as I did at Marlow Rowing Club. In fact, I saw him run once in a Russian red vest, which I loved even more, because I had one, too. I'd swapped shirts with a Russian rower at an event in Moscow in 1979 and wore it secretly on long-distance sculling races when I didn't think the organisers would notice. So to me, Ovett and I were kindred spirits.

Coe was a more aloof figure. He didn't register with me in the same way. He had his admirers, millions of them, astonished at his feats the year before Moscow, when he broke three middle-distance world records in 41 days – 800 metres, mile, 1500 metres. Meanwhile, Ovett was amassing an unbeaten record that stretched over nearly three years and over 40 races by the time they reached Moscow. They had tended to avoid one another in competition, but Moscow would be the definitive showdown. Both would race in the 800 metres, for which Coe was favouite, and the 1500, for which Ovett's more bullish style made him the favourite.

I was an Ovett man, because he was a bit of a rebel, like I am.

On the 800 metre start line, Coe had the knowledge that his personal best was a full second-and-a-half faster than anyone else's in the field. And what did that mean to him that day? Absolutely nothing. Instead he was dominated by doubt.

'In Moscow I was almost 24, but I'd been doubting I could beat him [Ovett] since I was 18, such was his stature. Losing the 800 metres in Moscow the way I did was a reflection of my inner self.' He didn't sleep the night before. He was just lying there 'listening to my own heartbeat. I have never known pressure like it.'

It would take a courageous effort to overturn the disappointment within days and come out to face a similar challenge against a rival, at his most comfortable distance, who had just beaten you at yours.

The media frenzy was intense. Over 400 journalists had attended Coe's first press conference in Moscow, and Britain was divided down the middle in allegiance to either man. Coe knew he could not, and should not, lose that 800 metre race. And yet he did lose, running the worst tactical race of his life from the back of the field. His father, mentor and coach, Peter, offered only one unprintable sentence of analysis after the race.

While Coe buckled, Ovett bolted to gold, and Coe, the golden boy, could claim only unwanted silver. I remember the headlines, dwelling with ghoulish interest on failure rather than celebrating Ovett's success.

It would take a courageous effort to overturn the disappointment within days and come out to face a similar challenge against a rival, at his most comfortable distance, who had just beaten you at yours. Lesser men would have faked a hamstring injury and caught the first plane home. But as Coe said himself, 'To come back in the 1500 metres against a guy who had won 42 straight races, as Steve had, demanded going deeper into the well …'

I have looked into that well at times. I know what he means. You learn about yourself in the half-hour before a race, when all the training has been done, when nothing and no one can help you dig out a performance but your own desire and determination. The worst I have ever felt before a race was probably in Atlanta, when Matthew and I had put ourselves in such an emotional straitjacket by predicting to the British media that we would win the gold medal. Boasting wasn't my style. We should have just shut up and rowed.

I never did it again, certainly not before Sydney when there was pressure enough from age, ill-health and the monumental challenge of winning a fifth successive gold medal. But in Atlanta, I must have had a glimpse of Coe's feelings as he emerged from the tunnel for the Moscow 1500 metres. No matter the records he held, no matter the times he was capable of running. All that was swept away in the past. All that counted was the next race. One race, one chance, to be a champion.

He sprinted ferociously for the line with 700 metres to run. It was an extraordinary finish. He completed the last 400 metres in 52.2 seconds, the last 100 metres in 12.1 seconds. His face as he crossed the finish line, the new Olympic 1500 metre gold medallist, betrayed his feelings. He was experiencing his own salvation.

And Ovett? All too clearly, if you look at his relatively untroubled expression, here was a man who had achieved his dream. He had already won his Olympic gold medal, just not in the event he expected. He admitted later that his victory in the 800 metres had just fractionally reduced his motivation. In élite sport, a fraction is all it takes to change the course of history.

> *You learn about yourself in the half-hour before a race, when all the training has been done, when nothing and no one can help you dig out a performance but your own desire and determination.*

Nadia Comaneci

Montreal 1976
Gymnastics

The only thing that Nadia Comaneci and I have in common (I have never done the splits for a start) is that we were both 14 in 1976. In her case, she was at the Montreal Olympics scoring the first-ever perfect 10 in gymnastics. I was at home, climbing into a rowing boat for the first time with a bunch of my schoolmates. My first Olympics was eight years away. Nadia's career would be over by then, after a soaring and highly photogenic reign as a teenaged superstar.

The picture is amazing, living proof of how flexible and controlled the human body can be through endless, rigorous training. Flexibility was never my strong point. I can't touch my toes these days. I can just about reach my knees, and that's only because I have such long arms. But I understand the demands of training. I suffered, like most rowers, the miserable, cold grind of it all on those winter mornings when your nose hairs freeze and ice runs down the back of your neck. At least I was there because I wanted to be.

We were both 14 in 1976. In her case, she was at the Montreal Olympics scoring the first-ever perfect 10 in gymnastics. I was at home, climbing into a rowing boat for the first time.

In Nadia's case, being such a young girl from a totalitarian country that brooked no rebellion, the toll was far greater. She seldom smiled, they say she never cried, and at 15 she allegedly tried to commit suicide by drinking bleach. She subsequently claimed that she drank only shampoo as a 'cry for help', but neither course of action could be considered healthy.

She was the youngest Romanian to be awarded 'The Gold Medal of the Hero of Socialist Labour' by then-president and Communist dictator Nicolae Ceausescu, and her whole career seemed to involve heavy repression of freedom. It seems such a shame to me, someone who enjoyed sport so much as an addition to boring things like school, that she should have been so unhappy. She actually attended the 1984 Los Angeles Olympics, but only as a spectator, and only under the unsubtle scrutiny of her guardians. I certainly didn't come across her there, competing at my first Olympics. To be fair, I probably wouldn't have noticed.

She was the youngest Romanian to be awarded 'The Gold Medal of the Hero of Socialist Labour' by then-president and Communist dictator Nicolae Ceausescu, and her whole career seemed to involve heavy repression of freedom.

In my view, gymnastics is a different type of sport. It doesn't come under the heading of 'Citius, Altrius, Fortius' (faster, higher, stronger). I have a problem with any sport that's judged. I don't see how human judgement, with all the politics and prejudice involved, can produce universally acknowledged champions. I accept that Comaneci was a brilliant performer. You can see that with the naked eye. But there are too many fine lines and suspected instances of bias to be sure of the results in general.

If we are going to get into this discussion, and I appreciate it's controversial, I also have a problem with sports that allow weight categories. Lightweight rowing? My argument against that is you don't have four-foot-tall basketball players. Olympic sport should surely be about the best. So in a sport such as boxing, there should be only one weight. By my reckoning, the winner should be the last man or woman standing.

At least Nadia's story has a happy ending. The name remains synonymous in Olympic history with perfection. That's not a bad accolade to have. Very few athletes could lay claim to being perfect at their sport and I am certainly not one of them. I can only say there were moments when I felt I came pretty close. There were five of them, in a 20-year career, and four were Olympic races. That tells me something. The bigger the event, the better I performed. It happened three successive times at the Barcelona Olympics in 1992, in the heats, the semi and the final. It was bizarre really, because I had been so ill with colitis leading up to the Games and would go on to be very ill again afterwards. But a window of health opened and Matthew and I had the best experience of rowing we'd ever known. I can describe it no other way than to say it felt easy, like 'poetry in motion', or a dream.

It would be interesting to know whether Comaneci felt the same when she was achieving her perfect 10s at the Montreal Games. Her subsequent history would suggest that, if so, it was not enough to trade for such a disciplined childhood. In the winter of 1989, she defected from Romania, fleeing across the Hungarian border, wading through mud and ice to begin a new life in America.

I have a problem with any sport that's judged. I don't see how human judgement, with all the politics and prejudice involved, can produce universally acknowledged champions.

Mary Decker
Los Angeles 1984
3000 metres

There she goes, falling into the infield – one of the most infamous stumbles in the history of Olympic sport. Mary Decker Slaney was an American superstar at the 1984 Los Angeles Olympics. Small, thin, pretty, she was perfect fodder for the home nation hype machine, not least because she was a genuine world-class runner, having won a middle-distance double (the 1500 and 3000 metres) at the World Championships in Helsinki the year before the Games.

To add to the excitement, fate had granted her the perfect rival in Britain's Zola Budd, a slight and slightly bemused transplanted South African, who famously ran her races barefoot. I'm trying to remember if I knew Zola, since we were in the same British team, but the rowers were living separately, near the lake, and we had little to do with the rest of the team. Also, this was my first Olympics and, knowing me, I was completely oblivious of everything except food, sleep and competition.

I do think now it was ill-judged to have Zola Budd running for Britain. In those days, because we didn't perform very well at Olympic Games, it filled a vacuum, but I don't think we'd even consider doing the same thing today.

So often over-hyped Olympic contests fail to get off the ground. On this occasion, however, Budd versus Decker produced one highly dramatic moment that would dominate the Games and, to some extent, the rest of both athletes' lives. The clash and fall has been replayed, examined, judged and reassessed for years. Essentially, at the 1600-metre mark of the (now defunct) 3000 metres, Budd, who was slightly leading, and Decker, just behind her, running hard on the inside of the same lane, suffered an accidental collision. Budd stumbled, her left leg flew outwards as she tried to regain her balance, and Decker tripped over, injuring a hip muscle in the process, which prevented her from getting up again. Her spikes had cut deeply into Budd's left leg.

Decker lay there, sobbing, in an agony of frustration and anger. I do remember those pictures, replayed it seemed endlessly, as the American media sought to blame Budd very squarely for the incident. I didn't think much about it then. I had a gold medal to ponder instead. But, looking back, I don't have any sympathy with Decker at all about the accident itself.

It was her own naivete that caused the clash. She was the favourite, she had much more experience than Budd had, and one of the first rules of middle-distance running, where athletes aren't confined to lanes, is to keep yourself out of trouble. There was a responsibility on her side to do that, especially as she was 26 at the time. Budd was just a kid, eight years younger, and she finished the race in seventh place, clearly devastated, in tears and bleeding, having been booed from all sides of the stadium.

I don't begrudge Decker her tears. Those I do understand. Crying in fury when you fail at an Olympics is more than just a brat throwing a tantrum. It is to do with the loss of something truly momentous to you at the time. Mary Decker believed, going into her home Games, that this was to be her crowning, her defining, moment. She was favourite, she was a two-time reigning world champion, she had endured a torrid childhood, many operations and injuries, some of which had kept her out for a full year of competition, and she had missed the two previous Olympics, one with injury, the second because of a political boycott completely beyond her control. But now, here, at home in the States, she had this one chance, one day, one race in which to make good all that had gone before.

And in a split second, it was gone; taken away, she felt. Her alleged rude ungraciousness to a grovelling Budd was a symptom of her sense of let-down. A more mature, rounded

I do think now it was ill-judged to have Zola Budd running for Britain. In those days, because we didn't perform very well at Olympic Games, it filled a vacuum.

person would have accepted the apology and said, as she did many years later, 'The reason I fell, some people think she [Budd] tripped me deliberately. I happen to know that wasn't the case at all. The reason I fell is because I am, and was, very inexperienced in running in a pack.'

But then sport doesn't manufacture mature, rounded people. It makes obsessives and she was most definitely one of them. She had one dream that day and when it was destroyed, sobbing and ill-temper seemed a reasonable response to her.

I speak from experience. Not that I sobbed, but I have been furious in my time. When it transpired that I would not be competing at the Moscow Olympics because Britain, affected by the Western boycott, was sending a scaled-down team, I watched on television in a state of boiling frustration. I felt thoroughly cheated. I still do. All that dedication and focus on one goal and some politician could sweep it all away to make a point that's been exposed as utterly fraudulent years later. See, it still makes me angry now.

And, funnily enough, the other time that springs to mind is when I was a kid – even then – rowing with my three schoolmates, Bill, Clive and Pete. We were trying to get selected for the international junior championship in 1979 and a broken seat meant we failed. We knew it was our last opportunity to row together as a four, and I was devastated; so much so that when I was selected to go alone as a single sculler, it was no consolation at all.

Sport does this to people. All your focus, life, thought goes towards one goal. Mary Decker's response in Los Angeles is a living example of how it feels to be thwarted, ruthlessly, publicly and irrevocably. Welcome to the world of sport.

Mary Decker believed, going into her home Games, that this was to be her crowning, her defining, moment.

Eric the Eel

Sydney 2000
100 metre freestyle

This is fantastic. In some ways, this epitomises the Olympic ideal. An unknown 'swimmer' arrived in Sydney from Equatorial Guinea, his proud country's single representative in the 100 metre freestyle, and basically, he couldn't swim.

Eric Moussambani, it turned out, had been practising in a hotel swimming pool back in Africa and had never been in an Olympic-sized pool in his life. He must have seen the water stretching into the distance in Sydney's famous aquatic centre – the very place where Ian 'Thorpedo' Thorpe had been hailed a human shark in his full-length racing suit – and wondered what on earth he was doing there.

In his first (and last) heat, he dived in and crawled, literally, through the water. His rivals had finished their swim when he was barely at the turning point. Painstakingly, gasping for breath and very, very slowly, he crawled back down his lane and, to

'The most important thing in the Olympic Games is not to win but to take part, just as the most important thing in life is not the triumph but the struggle. The essential thing is not to have conquered but to have fought well.'
The Olympic oath

the popping of flash bulbs and world acclaim, he completed his task in 1 minute 52.72 seconds, twice the time it took the other athletes in the race. Eric the Eel was born.

You might expect me to question his inclusion. I don't do anything of the sort. He didn't achieve the minimum entry requirements for the event, but the IOC have it in their power to award wild cards to encourage the developing nations. Eric was a beneficiary of the scheme and so wonderful was his reception and obvious his delight, it did nothing but enhance the magic of the Games.

I'll always remember an Indian skier at the Sarajevo Olympics in 1984, who missed a gate on the downhill run and then side-stepped back up again to take it properly. He looked like a beginner on a dry slope in Telford. I couldn't believe my eyes. But I give him huge credit for having the courage to take part.

Those are the important words to me – take part. It is a sharp reminder that the Olympic oath has genuine meaning: 'The most important thing in the Olympic Games is not to win but to take part, just as the most important thing in life is not the triumph but the struggle. The essential thing is not to have conquered but to have fought well.'

All right, I didn't mean them when I was competing at the Olympics. I wanted to win. But, honestly, had I ever been beaten by a better crew, I would have been disappointed but not inconsolable. For me, the point was to be the best I could be. If I had taken part and left every single particle of effort out there on the course, but been beaten, I would have had nothing to regret.

So wonderful was his reception and obvious his delight, it did nothing but enhance the magic of the Games.

If only the best turned up, you would have the powerful few so dominant that huge parts of the globe would be unrepresented. What would be the fun in that?

Eric gave it all he had, and he must be as proud of his Olympic appearance as any athlete who has ever competed in the Games. That is what makes this a truly global event. If only the best turned up, you would have the powerful few so dominant that huge parts of the globe would be unrepresented. What would be the fun in that?

Eric was pure fun. I can remember his closing few strokes, when he almost looked as though he was treading water. He was hardly moving at all.

The purists aren't always happy. I met Eddie the Eagle, our hapless ski jumper, at the Winter Games in Calgary in 1988, and he's quite a character. He didn't so much perform a jump as a flop, so brief was his time in the air, but who remembers who won? Everyone remembers Eddie.

I think that's why his shallow media celebrity was resented by various people, including members of the British team, and it was certainly a cause for reconsideration of entry qualifications by the IOC. They thought it made a mockery of the event (incidentally, won by Matti Nykanen of Finland) but I enjoyed his brief parabola across the Olympic landscape. If the Olympics ever lost its capacity for variety, sport would be poorer for it.

Birgit Fischer

Moscow 1980 to Athens 2004
Kayak

There is an obvious reason I find this German athlete's record such a source of interest. Look at the medals: gold in Moscow 1980, double gold in Seoul 1988, gold in Barcelona 1992, gold in Atlanta 1996, double gold in Sydney 2000, gold in Athens 2004. I make that eight gold medals, seven of them at five consecutive Olympics (she won two in Seoul). Makes my haul look pretty small by comparison, and the insult added to injury is that I tried kayaking once and fell in within four seconds.

Fischer's tally of eight gold medals over six different Olympics is a record she shares with Aladar Gerevich, the Hungarian fencer who managed the same total of golds over seven Olympic Games. She twice represented East Germany (interrupted by the boycott of 1984), then four times competed for the reunified Germany. After both the 1988 and 2000 Olympics, she announced her retirement (shades of me), only to return for the subsequent Games. She has been both the youngest-ever and oldest-ever Olympic canoeing champion, aged 18 and 42.

I look at that and wonder, could that have been me? I nearly went to Moscow at the age of 18. I would have done but for the Western boycott after the Russians invaded Afghanistan. (Don't get me started on politics.) And don't think I didn't seriously consider coming back at

I make that eight gold medals, seven of them at five consecutive Olympics (she won two in Seoul). Makes my haul look pretty small by comparison, and the insult added to injury is that I tried kayaking once and fell in within four seconds.

the age of 42 in Athens. It was only the sight of my coach, Jurgen, slowly and meaningfully shaking his head that nipped the plan in the bud.

So I have great admiration for this sportswoman, while acknowledging that the Army Sports Club in Potsdam, where she was coached when she was growing up, would have had one of the most sophisticated regimes in the world. She worked as a sports instructor in the East German Army, attaining the rank of major by the time the Berlin Wall came down in 1990.

I have never met her, but I wonder if she had difficulty readjusting to normal life once her sporting career was over, especially since it was so lengthy. Even before she retired she was looking for other things to do. In 1999, she stood, unsuccessfully, as a candidate for a centre-right liberal party in elections for the European parliament.

I can honestly say that, unlike Birgit and Seb Coe, I have never really been drawn to politics as a career. (See my comment above.) Obviously, there are times when the lines blur. It is inevitable when you have a voice and you are passionate about something that you develop a campaigning state of mind. But politics obliges you to say things you don't mean, and I would be terrible at that.

That doesn't mean I have been unimpressed by certain political individuals. When I was chairman of the Athletes' Advisory Board during the London Olympic bidding process, I could make contact with the then prime minister, Tony Blair,

She worked as a sports instructor in the East German Army, attaining the rank of major by the time the Berlin Wall came down in 1990.

In the early days of the Olympic bidding process, it was evident the government didn't want to bid because they thought they were going to lose to Paris. I passionately believed they should bid anyway, win or lose, to raise the profile of British sport.

whenever I needed to, and he would often call me at short notice for a photo shoot in the garden of Number 10. I was allowed to park behind the house and go in the back way. I was rather hoping I'd have the same space when I watched the Olympic beach volleyball on Horse Guards Parade, but something told me it wouldn't be available any more.

The most interesting thing about politics sometimes is understanding the unspoken agenda. In the early days of the Olympic bidding process, it was evident the government didn't want to bid because they thought they were going to lose to Paris. I passionately believed they should bid anyway, win or lose, to raise the profile of British sport. But I remember clearly one meeting with Tessa Jowell MP, who became Labour's minister for the Olympics, when – reading between the lines – my interpretation of what she was asking was, 'What can we offer British sport as a sweetener for not bidding?'

Fortunately, a survey came out so overwhelmingly in favour of bidding for the Olympics, and newspapers including the *Telegraph* mounted such a positive campaign, the government changed its mind.

All in all, I think it is better for sports people like myself to remain non-political.

Cathy Freeman

Sydney 2000
400 metres final

I look at this picture and all I can see is a woman who is being comforted after losing. She looks distraught. In fact, nothing could be further from the truth. This was Cathy Freeman's moment, seconds after victory in the Olympic 400 metres in front of an ecstatic home crowd. It was the pinnacle of her career, the successful culmination of her dream to win for her country, Australia, and her people, the Aboriginal race. On the shoulders of one slim woman in a green catsuit rested the political and social redemption of a nation. It was almost a ridiculous burden. Her achievement reminds me of the first moonwalk. One short run for an athlete, one giant leap (and a party) for Aussie-kind.

Her face, her apparent pain, reminds me of Los Angeles and my first Olympic gold medal, aged 22, in the coxed four, when first I felt relief, and then I found myself thinking, 'Is that it?' I hadn't planned the aftermath. I didn't know what to feel, do, think, anything. You cross the line, you win Olympic gold, you ought to be 'happy'. But, in my experience, it's never as simple as that. Remember me after Atlanta, pleading to be shot if I ever went near a boat again.

I don't ever remember being as sad as Cathy looks in the picture. But when we crossed the line in Sydney for my fifth gold medal, two days before Cathy's monumental victory in the Olympic Stadium, I wasn't exactly ecstatic. If you look at the pictures of me after the race,

> *I didn't know what to feel, do, think, anything. You cross the line, you win Olympic gold, you ought to be 'happy'. But, in my experience, it's never as simple as that.*

there was no celebration, no elation. It didn't occur to me to dive into the lake, as Matthew did. (I didn't have the energy for one thing.) I had simply equalled my expectation and the expectation of others upon me. Mainly, I felt relief, and later, satisfaction; but never was there ecstasy.

When you are an Olympic athlete, you focus on one day for four years, and the closer it gets, the harder it gets. Every part of your existence is gearing up for *that* day, *that* time, *that* race. You do other things, of course. Try to find sponsors, play a bit of golf, fall asleep on the sofa, but that one race is never out of your mind. The pressure builds and builds, and if you are expecting to win, and if a whole country is expecting you to win, you can do only one of two things – equal the expectation or fail.

Cathy had equalled expectation. She was probably feeling the pure relief of knowing she had finished the job and let no one down. She was being relieved of her burden. 'I was totally overwhelmed because I could feel the crowd all around and all over me,' she explained later. 'So I had to sit down and make myself feel normal and get comfortable.'

In my case, going into Sydney, I still expected to win. I was, as the newspapers reminded me leading up to the Games, potentially too old, potentially too ill and visibly less of a physical specimen than I had been in my prime. I was 38 and had been an established diabetic for three years. To be absolutely honest,

'I was totally overwhelmed because I could feel the crowd all around and all over me. So I had to sit down and make myself feel normal and get comfortable.'
Cathy Freeman

When you are an Olympic athlete, you focus on one day for four years, and the closer it gets, the harder it gets. Every part of your existence is gearing up for that day, that time, that race.

I didn't know whether my body would survive the race. But the one thing I did have was belief. So despite what anybody else thought, I still expected to win. We won. I was satisfied. Where is the elation in that?

The exact polar opposite feeling was being experienced at the time by Marie-Jose Perec of France, reigning Olympic 400 metre champion and Cathy's leading rival. As Cathy, with superhuman calm, readied herself for race day, the Frenchwoman was demonstrating wildly erratic behaviour and eventually fled home from Sydney before the showdown. They said she had suffered a psychological breakdown. She said she had been threatened by a stranger in her hotel room.

As a fellow athlete, I believed neither explanation. She had simply lost belief in the fact she could win. It was hardly surprising. She had suffered from the Epstein Barr viral condition in 1998 and raced only infrequently in 1999. I believe she was simply under-prepared and she didn't want to humiliate herself. So she left. The President of the French Athletics Association accused her of leaving 'like a thief'. I think differently. Her belief had left her and she had little choice but to follow it home.

As for Cathy, there were some carping voices that her winning time of 49.11 seconds was inferior to the 48.63 she had recorded in Atlanta behind Perec's Olympic record. To that I say, so what? She did what she had to do to win.

GB Men's Hockey Team
Seoul 1988

This, to me, was the greatest GB team moment in Britain's Olympic history. I say that for two reasons – one because I was there and the celebrations were fantastic; and two because, in the best possible way, it was the triumph of an Olympic ideal. The GB hockey team were amateurs, and I mean that as the highest compliment. While Ben Johnson, at these same Olympics, was demonstrating the squalor of cheating, the hockey team were a group of men who had day jobs, family, working lives, and yet sacrificed their time and energy to bond as a unit that would become the Olympic gold medallists. I have every admiration for them. I know how hard it was to train every day as a full-time athlete. Their climb was even steeper and more daunting.

Among the players in the team you had a bank worker, a surgeon, a teacher, a newspaper shop proprietor and a former player on the satellite tennis circuit. None of them earned a living from sport. All of them, without exception, gave everything they had to be the best athletes they could be on the day.

In the best possible way, it was the triumph of an Olympic ideal. The GB hockey team were amateurs, and I mean that as the highest compliment.

After this moment, Ann and I, and a large bunch of other GB athletes, invaded the pitch to celebrate with the guys. Some of the players even remember seeing me there.

I like this picture because it truly tells the story – the devastation of the loser, the German player sunk on his knees in despair; the exhaustion, even bewilderment, of the winner, likewise on his knees but in a fog of different feelings; and, in the middle, the celebrating group. Here's a good trivia question. Who is the GB goalkeeper? Most people, I'm guessing, would say Ian Taylor, the teacher, who played regularly in goal at the time. In fact, the answer is reserve goalie, Veryan Pappin, an RAF man who jumped out of planes as his day job. The manager sent him on for the last 20 seconds of the match, just to give him the Olympic experience.

After this moment, Ann and I, and a large bunch of other GB athletes, invaded the pitch to celebrate with the guys. Some of the players even remember seeing me there. I know that David Faulkner, now performance director of GB hockey – the blond on his knees in the picture – remembers, and he tells a good story about that moment:

'I just collapsed at the final whistle. I don't really know why. Relief? Exhaustion? The enormity of such a long-held dream turning into reality? I think what was flashing through my mind – this may sound ridiculous – was a bloke I'd met in a park in Fareham before the team left for the holding camp in Hong Kong. I'd been training on my own, conducting shuttle runs between trees conveniently staked five yards apart by the local authority, when this guy came past walking his dog. He stopped.

"Oh, that's pretty impressive," he said.

"Yeah, well, I'm going to the Olympic Games tomorrow," I told him.

"Get away," he said and laughed, completely dismissing it as a joke. Irrationally, that was what I was thinking about as I sat on my knees on the pitch in Seoul – "If that bloke could see me now!" '

I understand David's reaction. The mind does not always behave rationally in the emotional release that pours out after victories. Remember my 'shoot me' quote in Atlanta (the only time in my life I've joined Muhammad Ali in Great Sporting Quotations anthologies).

The funny thing was, we must have had a sense that something major was going to happen at the hockey stadium that day. The match coincided with the final day of athletics on the track, which is normally the hot ticket for the other athletes. Peter Elliott was running in the 800 metres, and would come an agonising fourth, just out of the medals, but when I turned up at the hockey stadium with Ann, it was packed with other British athletes.

The Germans were probably favourites. They had already beaten GB in the preliminary round, but our team had then defeated India and the Soviet Union to reach a semi-final against the Australians, which they won 3–2. Something felt as though it might be brewing, and it was. Final score: GB 3 Germany 1. And it didn't even go to penalties.

For completeness, and because I love trawling through records and coming up with stray facts, to the irritation of everyone around me, here is the gold-medal-winning 1988 GB men's hockey team: Ian Taylor, David Faulkner, Paul Barber, Jonathan Potter, Richard Dodds, Martyn Grimley, Stephen Batchelor, Richard Leman, James Kirkwood, Kulbir Bhaura, Sean Kerly, Robert Cliff, Imran Sherwani, Russell Garcia, Veryan Pappin, Stephen Martin.

The mind does not always behave rationally in the emotional release that pours out after victories.

Aladar Gerevich
Los Angeles 1932 to Rome 1960
Fencing

If I had been a gold-medal-winning athlete for as long as this Hungarian fencer, my last Olympics would have been London 2012. What a thought that is! I would have been 50 years old – as he was in Rome. Obviously his body held up a little better than mine, but then he probably hadn't bashed his about as much as I did.

Gerevich competed in six successive Olympics from 1932, Los Angeles, to Rome in 1960, with an enforced break in the middle for the Second World War. At every single one, he succeeded in winning a gold medal in the sabre team event, and medals of different colours (gold, silver and bronze) as an individual. I ought to feel competitive about him. I managed gold at five straight Olympics, but he carried on for six.

Actually, it is quite difficult to dislike the guy. From the snippets of history that have been handed down, he sounds like the sort of stubborn, self-believing athlete you have to be to become, and continue as, a champion. In 1960, the Hungarian Fencing Committee told him that he was too old

Gerevich competed in six successive Olympics from 1932, Los Angeles, to Rome in 1960, with an enforced break in the middle for the Second World War.

to compete in Rome. Rather than going quietly, a middle-aged man past his sell-by date, he challenged every other member of the sabre team to an individual match – and beat them all.

I'm not going to be too hard on myself. That kind of longevity would be impossible in a sport as physical as rowing. My greatest historical competitor in that field would be Jack Beresford, the most famous oarsman this country has ever produced, until the modern crop came along. Born in 1899, he won medals at five Olympics, exactly the same as I did, but thankfully for my vanity, two of the five were silvers.

He was the British flag-bearer in Berlin, but perhaps his most famous moment was the incredibly close race he sculled against an American, John B. Kelly Snr, in Antwerp in 1920, just after the First World War. That single scull race went down as one of the closest finishes in Olympic rowing history, won by a whisker by the man from Philadelphia.

If I had been a gold-medal-winning athlete for as long as this Hungarian fencer, my last Olympics would have been London 2012. What a thought that is! I would have been 50 years old – as he was in Rome. Obviously his body held up a little better than mine, but then he probably hadn't bashed his about as much as I did.

I'm not going to be too hard on myself. That kind of longevity would be impossible in a sport as physical as rowing.

There is a postscript to that story. John B. Kelly Snr, while being one of America's greatest ever rowers, was not allowed to compete at Henley. It was rumoured this was because he worked in 'trade', something Henley Royal Regatta could not possibly tolerate in those days. 'Tradesmen' were considered as having an unfair advantage due to their development of muscle. It was also downright snobbery. Whatever the cause, he was banned.

What great revenge he was to enjoy! When I won at Henley in 1981, the admired VIP who presented me with my medal was his daughter, the late Grace Kelly, the American film actress who had gone on to become Princess Grace of Monaco.

Florence Griffith Joyner

Seoul 1988
100 metres and 200 metres

Cover up the head in this picture, and you could be looking at the muscular frame of a man. So great was the suspicion surrounding 'Flo-Jo' that I don't remember there being any great celebration of her remarkable sprint double victory in the 100 and 200 metres.

Admittedly, I was rarely aware of what was happening beyond the rowing lake, but even I – with the disqualification of Ben Johnson and the cloud of scepticism hanging over Flo-Jo – could tell the Olympic movement had hit a low point.

Tellingly, when mandatory random drug testing was introduced shortly afterwards, Flo-Jo's substantial frame melted away from the scene.

Perhaps this is a story of human temptation, and of what it does to a competitor to keep coming second. I was fortunate in my career. Coming second was not a torment I suffered very often, but I can see that a sportsman or woman, focused on winning and only winning, would find the continuous sense of failure unbearable. What you should do then is work harder. What some people did (and do) is cheat. It's human failing.

The trappings were female – the painted talons, the long flowing hair, the figure-hugging leotard – but the body definition had a muscle structure that belonged in a Mr Universe competition.

In individual sports, especially, whispered rumours about what other people are doing circulate all the time. Eventually, they can breed a sort of paranoia that if you're not doing something to enhance your performance, you'll be left behind. I've known athletes on the British team to have all sorts of lotions and potions (none of them illegal, I hasten to say) just to counterbalance that sense of being adrift of the pack. Those supplements develop almost magical properties in the athlete's mind – vitamin this, elixir of that – and it's because rumours of other chemical enhancements are so strong.

I think it's different in a team sport, such as rowing. We had each other to lean on. We also had a work ethic that made recourse to drugs unnecessary. We were prepared to half kill ourselves day after day to prepare. Maybe some characters are less willing to make that effort. We used to moan about the Eastern bloc and what they might be doing, but as long as we beat them, it didn't really matter. It is winning that counts, as Florence discovered.

Flo-Jo was the seventh of 11 children from a tough part of Los Angeles. She was a good athlete in her youth, but an eccentric character, if you believe the stories about her going out and about with a pet boa constrictor. At the age of 20 she was forced to drop out of athletics to earn a living, and despite coming back to win a 200 metre silver medal at the Los Angeles Games in 1984, she had to give up again in 1986, known as a perennial 'runner-up'. She was working as a bank teller and beautician when she decided to give it one last go.

The clue to what happened next may be the fact that she consulted the 'great' (and yet to be unmasked) sprinter, Ben Johnson. She apparently watched videos of his explosive starts from the blocks, but there remain suspicions that she went further into his preparations than that.

A new Griffith (by now married to the Olympic triple jump champion, Al Joyner) emerged. At the US trials for the

The clue to what happened next may be the fact that she consulted the 'great' (and yet to be unmasked) sprinter, Ben Johnson.

Seoul Olympics, she was a bridesmaid no longer. She ran 100 metres in a scorching 10.49 seconds, obliterating the veteran Evelyn Ashford's 1984 world record of 10.76 seconds. The trappings were female – the painted talons, the long flowing hair, the figure-hugging leotard – but the body definition had a muscle structure that belonged in a Mr Universe competition.

By the time she reached Seoul she was a centre of attention, but not necessarily for all the right reasons. In the 100 metres, she ran each round faster than the last, winning the event in 10.54 seconds. That time was faster than 12 of the men in their second-round heats and all of the men in the decathlon.

In the 200 metres, she twice broke the world record, first in the semi-final and then, two hours later, in the final with a time of 21.34. These figures, and her figure, were fuelling serious doubts. She didn't even look tired. Arms aloft and smiling, she was practically dancing as she crossed the finish lines. Shouldn't that kind of effort be hurting?

I didn't see her face-to-face in Seoul, but one of the rowing team did. He said she wore tons of make-up and that her face was really pitted. Typically, that is a sign of steroid abuse.

The circumstantial evidence mounted, but she got away with it; or perhaps she didn't. In 1998 she died in her sleep, aged 38, leaving behind a young daughter. An autopsy revealed that she had a congenital brain abnormality and that she had suffered an epileptic seizure and died as a result of asphyxiation.

I didn't see her face-to-face in Seoul, but one of the rowing team did. He said she wore tons of make-up and that her face was really pitted. Typically, that is a sign of steroid abuse.

Eric Heiden
Lake Placid 1980
Speed Skating

He's the man who sold me the idea of being a speed skater. I just haven't done it yet. But never say never. He was a huge, colossal figure at the Lake Placid Winter Olympics in 1980, and I mean that in every respect – thighs like a sprint champion and so great a favourite that one of his rivals was quoted as saying: 'We have no idea how to train to compete with him. We just wait for him to retire.' Now you know why I liked him so much.

The opposition were right. These were the Olympics when he entered all five speed-skating events – sprint and long track, from 500 to 10,000 metres – and won gold in all of them, breaking the Olympic record in four of them. In the 10,000 metres he broke the world record instead. I was completely hooked watching on television at home.

At some stage, a documentary about him was screened, how he grew up in Wisconsin and tied dusters to his feet to 'skate' around the shiny floors of his house. I expect a crack was made about how his mother didn't need to do the sweeping, but it wasn't his domestic talents that interested me.

Heiden carried the Stars and Stripes at the opening ceremony, and when he was measured for his ceremonial suit, the only trousers that could be found to accommodate his massive 29 inch thighs had a waist six inches too big for him.

He entered all five speed-skating events – sprint and long track, from 500 to 10,000 metres – and won gold in all of them.

In common with certain British five-times gold medallists, he was not entirely comfortable with the trappings of fame. He turned his back on what he called 'the great whoopee' and became an orthopaedic surgeon in Utah.

The only event for which he was not the clear favourite was the 500 metre sprint, which is always a lottery because of the risk of collision over such a short distance – plus he was up against the world record holder, Yevgeny Kulikov of the Soviet Union. But all fears proved groundless. He came off the final bend smoothly in the lead and stayed there. In the other four events, no one came close to beating him.

Even when he overslept before the 10,000 metres, because he had been up late watching the incredible US ice-hockey team's victory over the Soviet Union, his record remained untarnished – unless you count the fact he had to rush his breakfast.

He didn't linger in the sport. By 1985, he was the US Pro Cycling champion and the following year he competed in the ultimate test of cycling stamina, the Tour de France. He survived the climbs but crashed out five days from the finish.

In common with certain British five-times gold medallists, he was not entirely comfortable with the trappings of fame. He turned his back on what he called 'the great whoopee' and became an orthopaedic surgeon in Utah. It's quite a curious parallel. I'm an Olympic medallist and my wife is an orthopaedic doctor, a medical profession known affectionately in this house as 'butchery'.

Now I get on a soapbox. As well as admiration of the man, Heiden's story convinces me that Britain could be a far, far greater player at Winter Olympic sports if only we had just one arena dedicated to catering for sports on ice. Obviously, there aren't enough mountains and there isn't enough snow to give us a broad base of skiers or lugers, but we could house a training centre for skaters (figure, dance and speed), curlers and ice-hockey players, if only we had the vision to combine them all.

As it is, would-be ice-dance and figure-skating champions and speed skaters have to get up at about 3.30 a.m. to grab an hour on an ice rink miles away. It's crazy. We're skating with one hand tied behind our backs, whereas with a bit of planning and lottery funding, we could create one central base for all the winter sports needing a place to practise that isn't necessarily the Austrian Alps. Flat ice we can do.

Just as cycling has developed a brilliant record based on technology, great athletes and central training, so could many of the winter sports in this country. It just takes someone with the will and determination to seize the opportunity. I would love to present the case for such a facility. We talk about our Olympic legacy. How about this becoming a realised dream from the profits of the 2012 Olympics?

It might be too late for me. Perhaps my dreams of being a speed skater are unrealistic and, to be honest, my style is not well suited to bends. I tend to race as fast as humanly possible from one end of the rink to the other. Stopping is a matter of crashing into the barriers. I once found myself on an ice rink with a bunch of little Cub Scouts racing around, and the only way I could stop flattening one was to lift him up and put him down again as he accidentally crossed my path. Swerving was out of the question.

It's my upbringing. Rowers only ever work in straight lines.

Britain could be a far, far greater player at Winter Olympic sports if only we had just one arena dedicated to catering for sports on ice.

Walter Herrmann

Athens 2004
Basketball final

Here is a sporting ritual. This is Walter Herrmann, a member of the victorious Argentine Olympic gold-medal-winning basketball team at Athens in 2004, cutting off the basket at the end of the match to take home as a souvenir. Strictly speaking, this unofficial prize should have gone to teammate Luis Scola, who scored 25 points against Italy in the final, but at 6ft 9in Walter probably discovered that few people in life were disposed to argue with him.

It was a good day for Argentina. After a gold medal drought of 52 years, not only did they win the basketball final but their men's football team also came up with Olympic gold. No wonder they wanted a keepsake.

Strictly speaking, this unofficial prize should have gone to teammate Luis Scola, who scored 25 points against Italy in the final, but at 6ft 9in Walter probably discovered that few people in life were disposed to argue with him.

Matt Pinsent felt the same way at the Atlanta Olympics. He and I won the sole gold medal for Britain at those Games. It was hard won. I was at my grumpiest. It was there I begged the world to shoot me if I ever went near a boat again after winning the coxless pairs. But Matt's mind was whirling on other matters, as he watched the Union Flag raised to the sound of the national anthem during the medal ceremony.

How nice, he thought, and confided to me, if we should acquire that very flag and be allowed to keep it for posterity. The gold medal, of course, is the ultimate prize, but surely the flag that has been raised in your honour as you stand on the Olympic dais would be a very special souvenir indeed. That's what an Eton and Oxford education does for you. He's a deep thinker, Matt.

Sure enough, when we returned home to the UK, included in our luggage was the very same flag we'd so coveted, and which had kindly been given to us. I then made contact with a brilliant carpenter, who had made all my wooden cupboards at home, and suggested he might like to think about building a glass-fronted display case that could hold a large, precious, folded flag.

The gold medal, of course, is the ultimate prize, but surely the flag that has been raised in your honour as you stand on the Olympic dais would be a very special souvenir indeed.

Four years after its first appearance beside a lake in Atlanta, the flag had a second outing, this time overlooking the River Thames at Henley, to commemorate the deeds of four likely lads in Australia.

He came up with the very thing and there the flag rests to this day in the bar at the Leander Club, where we were based for so many years of our rowing careers.

As far as I know, it has been sprung from its case on just one occasion. In September 2000, Matt and I had just rowed to victory with James Cracknell and Tim Foster in the coxless fours finals in Sydney. My mind is in a whirl, and Matt, sharp as ever, is on the phone to the Leander Club. He suggested they might like to take out the flag and run it up the Leander flagpole in honour of the occasion half the world away. They were happy to comply. So four years after its first appearance beside a lake in Atlanta, the flag had a second outing, this time overlooking the River Thames at Henley, to commemorate the deeds of four likely lads in Australia.

Kelly Holmes
Athens 2004
Double middle-distance champion
800 metres final

Sheer shock. That is what her face registers. Sheer, unbridled, stunned surprise that she, Kelly Holmes, age 34, British middle-distance veteran, more familiar with stretchers, operating tables, crutches, bandages and lay-offs, had just become the Olympic 800 metre champion in Athens, beating her training partner and favourite for the title, Maria Mutola of Mozambique. It was almost a hurdle race, so many mental barriers had she to overcome.

So that would be it. One glorious gold medal with which to walk into the sunset. Satisfied, happy, she could treat the upcoming 1500 metres as a four-times-round lap of honour rather than a race. Her goal – her gold medal – had already been achieved.

This is why I admire Kelly so much. It was no such thing. Despite her gold, despite the overturning of every disappointment she had ever known in her life, she walked on to the track for the 1500 metres final still the same furiously competitive athlete she had ever been. Her mental toughness

Many times in sport, people don't get what they deserve. Understandably, when things go wrong, as they do for all athletes sometimes, they slink away and give up.

> *'It would have been easy to spend the day off between the semi-final and final looking at what she had already done rather than looking ahead to the battle still to be fought.'*
> **Sebastian Coe**

was truly awesome as she dominated the race with tactical commonsense and a blistering burst of speed at the finish. The former nearly girl of British athletes was now a double Olympic gold medallist, and at those particular distances, the feat had previously been achieved by just four people – Albert Hill (Great Britain) in 1920, Peter Snell (New Zealand) in 1964, Tatyana Kazankina (Soviet Union) in 1976 and Svetlana Masterkova (Russia) in 1996. She was in rarefied company.

Her achievement compares and contrasts so much with what happened when one of my all-time favourite athletes, Steve Ovett, was in a similar situation. When Steve won his unexpected gold in Moscow in the 800 metres, overthrowing the favoured Seb Coe (very much a mirror image of Kelly's experience), it seemed crucially to diminish his drive. A change had come over him. I'm guessing that his hunger was satisfied. Kelly was entirely the opposite.

The way she conducted herself was remarkable. She dealt with the media interest and excitement. She dealt with the knowledge that she was sleeping with a gold medal right beside her bed. As Seb Coe said at the time, 'It would have been easy to spend the day off between the semi-final and final [of the 1500 metres] looking at what she had already done rather than looking ahead to the battle still to be fought.'

Maybe Kelly just understood battles. She had, after all, been an army fitness instructor.

I suppose you can be practical about it. You can say that for the first time in her life she had been training at the highest possible level, joining the remarkable champion, Mutola, in Africa as a live-in training partner. But this could also be seen as a psychological disadvantage, given her proximity to a runner who had won all but one of her previous 38 races.

I also happen to believe that Kelly is one of those people who is very, very, very competitive.

I also happen to believe that Kelly is one of those people who is very, very, very competitive. I have met her many times now, since Athens, and we get on really well. I have seen, first-hand, what she is like when she takes part in anything like a sporting event.

We once both competed in a motor race at Silverstone, for fun, in awful conditions of pouring rain. I was plodding around hoping to survive, while Kelly roared off so fast that she went off into the gravel and had to be pulled out. Ultimately though, while I finished back in the field, she came second or third.

Even in the TV series *Superstars*, when she was up against World Cup rugby winner Mike Catt in a 1500 metre race, I saw her race-face. 'Oh, I'm not fit,' she said, but you could tell she was really, seriously intent on winning. It wouldn't be easy against a strong man, even though it was her speciality. She beat him by a hair's breadth. She did it by sheer guts and determination. She's got bundles and bundles of that.

Many times in sport, people don't get what they deserve. Understandably, when things go wrong, as they do for all athletes sometimes, they slink away and give up. Kelly must have felt like that many times. I remember the story about her throwing her spikes away in a dustbin after yet another injury had wrecked her race. But there is an old-fashioned virtue that doesn't get much respect in these days of instant gratification. It is called 'perseverance', and if ever an athlete embodied that concept, I have to say it is Kelly Holmes.

Israeli Hostage Crisis
Munich 1972

What would I have done? Had I been an athlete in the Olympic Village at Munich on 5 September 1972, when news spread like wildfire that terrorists had murdered two Israeli athletes and were holding nine more hostage, what would my reaction have been? The chilling sight of a hooded figure, captured momentarily on camera, makes me wonder.

This event remains the most barbaric act in Olympic history, made all the worse by the perpetrators using those most innocent of any perceived crime to further their twisted political aims.

It upsets me how often sportsmen and women become caught in a political crossfire. I was furious and frustrated in 1980 when, having qualified for the Moscow Olympics as an 18-year-old, I couldn't go because of the Western boycott of the Games in the Soviet Union. Rowing did send a team, but a vastly reduced one and there was no room for me.

This event remains the most barbaric act in Olympic history, made all the worse by the perpetrators using those most innocent of any perceived crime to further their twisted political aims.

German marksmen were waiting to kill the terrorists on sight, but the rescue attempt was bungled. Only three terrorists were killed. The remaining five slaughtered every one of the hostages.

But Munich was different. The 11 Israeli athletes and coaches who died that day were victims of a terrifying atrocity that moved hour-by-hour to a bloody culmination. Those were the days when the Olympic Village was surrounded by a token wire fence. It was the work of minutes for six pro-Palestine terrorists in tracksuits to break through and join two colleagues already inside. At 4 a.m. they burst through the doors of the Israeli accommodation, Block 31, and instantly murdered a wrestling coach and a weightlifter in a hail of bullets. Ten Israelis escaped in the confusion, nine were held as hostages.

A typewritten ultimatum was dropped from the balcony, demanding, in English, the release of 236 prisoners in Israel. They threatened to murder a hostage every hour if their demands were not met. The Israeli prime minister, Golda Meir, refused.

There followed an afternoon of negotiations. Helicopters were summoned to transfer terrorists and hostages to a local airfield where a plane was waiting to fly them to Cairo. It was a trap. German marksmen were waiting to kill the terrorists on sight, but the rescue attempt was bungled. Only three terrorists were killed. The remaining five slaughtered every one of the hostages. The next day, a memorial service was held before the Games continued. No Arab state, nor the Soviet Union, sent a representative.

I was 10. I have only a vague memory of something going on. It stands testament to the power of the human desire to compete that the Games bounced back and Mark Spitz, a man who in part inspired my own Olympic story, went on to create history in the Olympics' darkest hour. Looking back from the vantage point I have now does make me wonder what I would have done as an athlete had I been in Munich that day.

We know a little bit about how they felt then. One athlete at the time was quoted as saying: 'Don't ask me, I'm in tomorrow's semi-finals.' Even Jesse Owens reportedly said: 'The Games must not be cancelled. That would be surrender.'

Who am I to say I wouldn't have said and felt exactly the same? I have some idea, though. In Atlanta, overnight, just before the pairs final in which Matt and I would be rowing for my fourth, his second, Olympic gold medal, a bomb went off in a park in the city. We woke up to the news. No one knew if anyone, or how many, had died. We didn't know until much later that one person – and that's one too many – had died.

I questioned myself that morning. Did I really want to row in a race when an atrocity of unknown proportions had taken place at the same event? Perhaps I surprised myself. I know there are times when I mistake sport for a life-and-death struggle, but it isn't. You have to be aware of your humanity.

In the end, I thought this: 'The Games haven't been cancelled, so someone today is going to get on that lake and row for the Olympic gold medal and be Olympic champion, in which case, why shouldn't that someone be me?'

Did I really want to row in a race when an atrocity of unknown proportions had taken place at the same event?

Knud Enemark Jensen

Rome 1960
100 kilometre team time trial

How does it end like this? A man with a fractured skull being carried off the road, his bicycle toppled on its side, an ambulance racing towards him, too late. He dies in a Roman hospital hours later. An autopsy discovers a cocktail of drugs in his body.

Let me try to explain, because I cannot condemn him outright. As an athlete, I understand how easy it is for distorted thinking to take you to a place of no return.

This man was a Danish cyclist, who was certainly not alone in believing his only chance of winning, of performing well, was to enhance the effort with drugs. The autopsy on his body discovered amphetamines in his system, as well as a drug called Roniacol, a flushing drug that could lower blood pressure. Eventually, it came to light that he had also taken eight pills of another drug, phenylisopropylamine, and 15 pills that combined caffeine with amphetamines. On that cocktail of drugs, he was an accident waiting to happen.

This man was a Danish cyclist, who was certainly not alone in believing his only chance of winning, of performing well, was to enhance the effort with drugs.

> *Only one in 10,000 individuals in this country are good enough to become Olympic athletes. Of that élite corps, only a small percentage become the ultimate – a gold medallist.*

The doctors subsequently agreed that the direct cause of his crash was the heat, not the drugs, but it makes you wonder whether the chemicals inside him exerted their own influence on his body and mind.

Why would an Olympian risk such a thing? Here is why. Only one in 10,000 individuals in this country are good enough to become Olympic athletes. Of that élite corps, only a small percentage become the ultimate – a gold medallist. And yet those individuals have worked 10, 20 years, unceasingly, devotedly, devouringly, for that tantalising prize.

When I rowed at the Olympics, I wanted to win. That six minutes of my life seemed so crucial, it developed an importance beyond reason. It would either be my crowning moment or a moment of despair. I didn't look beyond it. Every second of all four years that had gone before were going be vindicated, or not, by what happened next. It shouldn't be like that, but in the grip of competitive desire, that is how an athlete feels. If they felt less committed, I don't think they'd stand a chance.

I remember Matt Pinsent saying to me once that if someone gave him the option of trading in all his world championship victories and all the Olympic medals he had already won, just to guarantee the next Olympic gold, he'd do it. He'd snap their hand off. That is how much the next one always matters in the mind of an athlete.

I was one of the lucky ones. I have failed at many things, but I never did feel the despair of Olympic failure, nor a sense of hopelessness in competition. But for those people who did, the temptation to seek help by whatever means possible is completely explicable.

As for sport in 1960, there was no drugs ban. Jensen was able, and maybe felt entitled, to seek help where he could, and history

I was one of the lucky ones. I have failed at many things, but I never did feel the despair of Olympic failure, nor a sense of hopelessness in competition. But for those people who did, the temptation to seek help by whatever means possible is completely explicable.

suggests that performance enhancers were common in his sport. At least his terrible death helped prompt the debate about athletes taking drugs, and the bans came in within a decade.

A good thing, too. While my understanding of drug cheats is real, I hate what it does to sport. If we didn't try to put the brakes on the cheats, there is no limit to the freaks we could be chemically producing. I assume some athletes are taking drugs now. Perhaps, with modern technology, they think the risks are vastly reduced. Perhaps they are. But there is still the fact that they are destroying, if not their own bodies, the whole concept of sport.

I am grateful for the sake of sport, and especially the children we try to encourage into it, that drug bans exist and there is no free-for-all, whatever some of the libertarians may say. We can see in this picture where free-for-alls may get you – dying by a roadside at the age of 23. I can see now that no sporting moment, however great, is worth this destruction. I could see in my prime that drug abuse was not an option. But if I had been a nearly man, tantalised by a prize I couldn't reach by natural means, and surrounded by a drug-taking culture, would I have been so brave?

I like to think I would, but who knows themselves that well? I certainly don't blame Jensen. I feel very, very sorry for him.

Ben Johnson
Seoul 1988
100 metres final

I was there, actually in the Olympic Stadium, to watch one of the greatest moments in the history of the Games. It happened in a flash. I remember the cheers turning to gasps as we, the crowd, understood just how fast one superhuman had run – 100 metres in 9.79 seconds, the world record smashed to smithereens.

It was over 20 years later that I discovered I hadn't been there at all. I couldn't have been. I had a race myself at the rowing lake the next day. Andy Holmes and I had won the coxless pairs on the morning of Ben Johnson's race, but the next day we were going to try to add a second gold in the coxed pairs. There is no way I'd be so unprofessional as to go out the night before. I can't have done. And yet so great was the visual drama of that iconic, and tragic, 100 metre race, I put myself in the scene. It's bizarre. I can't rationalise it.

I remember the cheers turning to gasps as we, the crowd, understood just how fast one superhuman had run – 100 metres in 9.79 seconds, the world record smashed to smithereens. It was over 20 years later that I discovered I hadn't been there at all. I couldn't have been.

> *Johnson wasn't superhuman after all. He was just cheating.*

Perhaps the event was so momentous I imagined myself there; perhaps I saw it on television somewhere in the Olympic Village. I do know that I thought I was seeing something pretty special – one of the greatest explosions of athletic power ever. It was three days later we discovered he was accused of being a drugs cheat. The news went around the village like wildfire. I felt, first, profound shock. Then I was sickened and disappointed. I thought I'd been a witness to something truly special. It turned out to be false. Within days we had gone from the best to the worst sport can be.

Johnson wasn't superhuman after all. He was just cheating. It later transpired he'd been on anabolic steroids, and although he reportedly admitted taking performance-enhancing drugs, he denied taking Stanzobol, for which he tested positive. There had been those, including his rival Carl Lewis, who had their suspicions. He was known in certain athletic circles as 'Benoid' for his exaggerated muscle structure and telltale yellow eyes. Led by his coach, he had feared being a nearly man. The fear that rivals resorted to drugs, and the rewards of being an Olympic gold medallist, tempted him fatally.

I have never said I don't understand it; I just hate it as an attitude. If sport is to have any meaning at all, it's about testing your mental and physical prowess against that of somebody else. Chemical substances distort the battle. That's why I was always deeply unhappy about taking insulin at the 2000 Olympics in Sydney. As a diabetic, I needed it to keep me alive and it was approved by the IOC, but it was still a foreign substance. I had to have an outside ingredient to win my fifth gold medal. It wasn't all me. Admittedly, otherwise I'd die, but I've never felt entirely comfortable about that.

Johnson decided that a foreign substance, and a banned one, was worth the risk, but I cannot imagine how he felt as the clock ticked after his post-race drug test, knowing he faced disgrace and the ruination of his career. Perhaps he didn't know. Perhaps, since he had taken the steroid 26 days before, he thought it would be flushed out of his system already. But both the A and B samples came back positive and eventually the Canadian chef de mission had to go to him and request back his falsely awarded gold medal. 'We love you,' she said, 'but you're guilty.'

He denied it at first, but eventually testified to the truth under oath. They banned him for two years and stripped him of all his medals and records. He came back in time for the Barcelona Olympics, when I was rowing with Matt Pinsent, but I can barely remember him at all there. He was nothing like the enhanced athlete he had been. He didn't even make the final. He was caught again in 1993, and this time he was banned for life.

To me, this photograph is so revealing because it's so deceptive. All those famous athletes, including Carl Lewis, four times Olympic gold medallist in Los Angeles, Linford Christie, British champion, Calvin Smith, former world record holder, Dennis Mitchell, future Olympic gold medallist, left behind by the whirlwind in front of them. They look like a line of also-rans. Johnson, massive and muscular, is clearly out in front from the start. We thought it was a great step for humanity. It turned out to be a helping hand from chemistry. He was fired up, not by inspiration, but by the same stuff they gave cattle to fatten them for market – not quite as heroic as we thought at the time.

Funnily enough, five of the eight in the race were subsequently to have their own brush with drug scandals, including Britain's Linford Christie and even Lewis himself. That might be a mitigating circumstance in Johnson's 'crime', but not to me. I still look at his image and think, 'You cheat.'

The Canadian chef de mission had to go to him and request back his falsely awarded gold medal. 'We love you,' she said, 'but you're guilty.'

Michael Johnson
Atlanta 1996
Double sprint champion
200 metres final

He looks like he's flying, the 'Man in the Golden Shoes', Michael Johnson, winning the 200 metres in Atlanta, and looking back to check his time because, as he told me many years later, 'I knew it was good. I just didn't know how good.' He was wrong. It wasn't just good. It was stunning – 19.32 on the clock represented the monumental smashing of his own world record.

We were both at the Atlanta Olympics, him vying to become the first man on earth to win both the Olympic 400 and 200 metre finals and me feeling the pressure of trying to win my fourth Olympic gold medal. I didn't really know Michael then. To me, he appeared to be an arrogant Texan. Sometimes he would speak to people, sometimes he wouldn't. It was a measure of his status at the time that the Olympic authorities had sanctioned the switching of race schedules to accommodate his assault on both those Olympic titles. The golden shoes were all part of the image. That wasn't how I did things. I remember teammate James Cracknell once turning up to race in strange, over-the-head sunglasses. We told him not to be such an idiot. As far as I was concerned, the nonsense stopped when the race began.

But maybe Johnson was the one man who could get away with anything. He seemed to exude confidence and a sense of his own destiny. His domination of his rivals was almost total. He was unbeaten in 54 races at 400 metres before Atlanta and duly won the Olympic final by almost one full second over Britain's Roger Black. To this day, Roger insists that he has an Olympic gold medal. It just happens to be coloured silver. They weren't in the same race. There was Johnson's performance and

'19.32. That's not a time. It sounds like my dad's birthday.'

Ato Boldon

the rest of the field were in a secondary contest of their own.

The only irritants in Johnson's life at that point were external. On the same night as his feat in the 400 metres, Carl Lewis tied two remarkable Olympic records by winning the same event – the long jump – for the fourth time and earning his ninth gold medal. In addition, the French diva athlete, Marie-Jose Perec, won the women's 200 metres to achieve exactly the same feat as Johnson was attempting.

That merely spurred him on. By now, he was no longer thinking in terms of winning and losing. His career had taken him beyond that stage. Now it was about becoming the kind of athlete, the kind of achiever, who makes an indelible mark on the world. We've spoken about this since then, Michael and I, and it may sound like breathtaking arrogance, but it is how an athlete would think. In the end, it's about self-improvement. Once you reach the pinnacle of your sport, you want the challenge of being the very best athlete you can be. The titles, the races, the medals are incidental. They take care of themselves.

The 200 metres was a greater challenge to Johnson. Only two weeks before Atlanta, Frankie Fredericks, the great Namibian sprinter, had beaten him in Oslo. That might have been a mental setback to a lesser man. Johnson remembers seeing Fredericks walk past him in the Atlanta call-room, where the athletes gather before a race, and found his mind wandering in speculation about his opponent. He knew such ill-discipline could be fatal, so he switched instantly to his default position. He visualised himself, only himself, running the forthcoming race.

The pressure was there, but he expected it. He did nothing to relieve it. 'The only thing you can do about pressure is acknowledge it, live with it and know that you have done everything humanly possible to win the race before you turn up on the start line.' That was his belief. That was also mine.

He stumbled slightly coming out of the blocks, but recovered immediately. 'The first half of the race, the first 100 metres, was like the first half of my career – I just wanted to win. But by the second half of the race, I knew I'd won and then I wanted to do something special.' He certainly did that. I think the photo sums up perfectly his determination to see how fast he had run, arching backwards to read the clock and discovering he had beaten his own world record by a phenomenal 0.34 seconds.

After the race, having felt a slight twinge in a hamstring, he wrapped ice round his right leg. The US decathlete, Chris Huffins, was on the infield at the time and told the assembled media: 'The only thing that hurt his hamstring was the re-entry burn.' He was seen by his fellow athletes as virtually superhuman. Bronze medallist Ato Boldon marvelled: '19.32. That's not a time. It sounds like my dad's birthday.'

A few years later, we were destined to work together at the BBC and I was honestly wary that he would still be the arrogant man I'd imagined. Nothing is further from the truth. Like most athletes, he wore his sense of supremacy as a shield, to prevent other athletes from getting to him, and, more likely, to maintain his own belief in himself. He had no arrogance about him at all. Not with me. I have found him to be such a nice guy, I was even more surprised when he admitted to me that he, too, was a shy kid, like I was. He seems to exude confidence in everything he does, but he told me he was a quiet boy, wary of being exposed to embarrassment.

I think this is an important clue to his personality. Those most willing to devote themselves to the incessant, painful, often soulless business of training tend to be introverts. Extroverts want an audience. OK, yes, I had an audience at the Olympics. But would once every four years really do it for the theatrical types? Most of the time my crowd consisted of three other sweaty men, a swan and Jurgen on his bike.

'The only thing you can do about pressure is acknowledge it, live with it and know that you have done everything humanly possible to win the race before you turn up on the start line.'
Michael Johnson

Eric Liddell
Paris 1924
400 metres

I know that beach where they filmed *Chariots of Fire*. It is at St Andrews, just in front of the golf course – miles and miles of sand. All you need is a big slice and a cross wind … and you can almost make it with a really bad shot.

Perhaps partly as a legacy of the film, there is a romantic story attached to Eric Liddell, the devoutly Christian sprinter who won a gold medal in the 400 metres (440 yards in those days) at the Paris Olympics in 1924. It is popularly imagined, thanks to the scriptwriters, that he discovered the heats of the 100 yard dash, his speciality, would be run on a Sunday, therefore forcing his withdrawal, only when boarding the ferry to France.

In fact, he was aware of the schedule a good six months before the Olympics, and so while it is true he was delivering a sermon in a Scottish kirk in Paris while the race was being run in the Olympic Stadium, he had plenty of warning to devise an alternative plan.

He had banned himself from the 100 yards and the frustration, even though self-imposed, had spurred him on. He had entered the equivalent of our 200 metres and 400 metres instead.

At the Paris Olympics, the 400 metres contained a classier field of competitors, plus Liddell had been drawn in the unpopular outside lane. He set off at an electrifying, perhaps suicidal, pace.

I don't want to sound boring and pedantic, although I'm going to, but there is no way any athlete could move up from running short sprints to a full lap at Olympic level without preparation. They did have lactic acid in those days. It is a substance with which I was extraordinarily familiar for about 24 years of my life. I remember, even at school, having to walk down the stairs backwards because the training had left my muscles so stiff.

Liddell was probably an incredible athlete, and may have had guts and determination above the average. His tolerance to lactic acid may have been greater than most, but I don't believe any athlete on earth can ever override the chemical make-up of the human body.

It would be so tempting to see this story as an incident of divine intervention, but it was probably far more prosaic than that. Namely, he had six months to build up his tolerance to muscle fatigue. That would do it. He was a fine athlete, he *trained*, he won.

He had banned himself from the 100 yards and the frustration, even though self-imposed, had spurred him on. He had entered the equivalent of our 200 metres and 400 metres instead. In the 200, the 'Flying Scot' finished third, a creditable performance, but Liddell was not the type of man to feel satisfied with bronze. He had become famous the year before when, at an England/

Ireland meeting, he was knocked to the ground during a 440 yard race. By the time he had climbed to his feet, he was 20 yards adrift of the field, and yet, such was his ferocious pace and determination, he overhauled every man in front of him to win the race. Apparently, his post-race quote was simply: 'I don't like to be beaten.' That is a concept I well understand.

But at the Paris Olympics, the 400 metres contained a classier field of competitors, plus Liddell had been drawn in the unpopular outside lane. He set off at an electrifying, perhaps suicidal, pace, passing the halfway mark in a scarcely believable time of 22.2 seconds, only 0.3 seconds slower than he had run in the 200 metres final. His rivals must have been expecting him to blow up or tire dramatically, allowing them back in the race. Instead, he actually increased his lead and won by more than five metres.

The pace was so ferocious that two of his rivals stumbled and fell just trying to live with his speed. Liddell broke the Olympic record, and John Taylor, one of the US athletes in his wake, crawled over the line nearly 10 seconds behind him. It was, by any standards, an awesome feat and one that richly deserved the hero's welcome he received in Scotland. He was paraded around Edinburgh University, the Olympic garland around his head, in honour of the achievement.

Twenty-one years later, at the age of 43, he died of a brain tumour in a Japanese internment camp in Weifang, China, during the Second World War. But that isn't quite the end of the story. In 1991, a monument to Liddell was raised in Weifang, appropriately carved out of Scottish granite, upon which the biblical quotation was written: 'They shall mount up with wings as eagles; they shall run and not be weary.'

For absolute truth, there should be a rider to that quote: 'They shall run and not be weary … until the lactic acid kicks in.'

> *The pace was so ferocious that two of his rivals stumbled and fell just trying to live with his speed.*

This page: 1) Butlin's baby contest (aged six months, didn't win). 2) Some early monkey business with my sister Jane. 3) Me as a schoolkid about 5 years old. 4) On sister Christine's wedding day, 24th March 1973. 5) Slogging it out on the river. 6) School crew, left to right: Nicky Baatz, Clive Pope, Robert Hayley, me, Peter Meconnell. 7) Coxing a boat, left to right: Brian Scrivener, Adam Kin, me and me and me

This page: 8) The Diamond Challenge Sculls, Henley Royal Regatta, 1983. 9) Same Olympian, different pet (Tasha). 10) World Championships, Nottingham, 1986. 11) With family and MBE, 1987. 12) *Left to right*: Tim Foster, me, Matt Pinsent, James Cracknell, The Steward's Challenge Cup, Henley Royal Regatta, 1997. 13) With Ann and the children, Sydney 2000. 14) Receiving my Knighthood, 2001. 15) At the royal unveiling of my statue, Higginson Park, Marlow.

Vanderlei de Lima

Athens 2004
Marathon

As has been said in American politics, there are known knowns, there are known unknowns and there are unknown unknowns. This is undoubtedly a case of the latter.

When Brazilian marathon runner Vanderlei de Lima was preparing for his event at the 2004 Athens Olympics, he would have taken on board the heat, the hills, the adrenalin, the wall – every last facet of the 'known unknowns'. What he could not possibly have taken into account was a random attack by a defrocked Irish priest, who had already disrupted the running of the 2003 British Grand Prix by invading the track at Silverstone.

This bizarre and unwarranted intrusion in the marathon happened with only five miles to go, and the Brazilian was leading by a good 25 seconds over his nearest rivals. Perhaps he would have won, perhaps he wouldn't, but either way he was completely unprepared when Cornelius Horan came charging out of the crowd, dressed somewhat eccentrically, and to use a rugby term, 'bundled him into touch'. I just can't imagine the athlete's shock at that moment. He must have been completely bewildered.

Fortunately, a Greek spectator was clear-headed. He 'subdued', according to press reports, the errant former priest. I would love to know what that meant. A swift right hook would not have been out of place. Then he lifted the Brazilian to his feet and put him back into the race. His name, the Grecian saviour, was Polyvios Kossivas and de Lima was careful afterwards to offer him grateful thanks.

What he could not possibly have taken into account was a random attack by a defrocked Irish priest.

But at least 10 seconds, possibly more, of his lead had been swallowed by the incident and in the final few miles he was overtaken by two athletes, leaving him with the bronze medal. I know how I would have felt. Murderous, is probably fair. As de Lima said later, the worst of it was he had no idea of his attacker's intention. 'I was scared, because I didn't know what could happen to me, whether he was armed with a knife, a revolver or something, and whether he was going to kill me.'

He said he believed the attack cost him the gold medal, but he must be a thoroughly nice guy, with a very even temper, because he performed a small victory dance in his last few strides to denote his happiness at receiving a medal at all. In the end, he seemed to accept his extraordinary fate with such goodwill that the Olympic movement awarded him the Baron de Coubertin medal for sportsmanship.

He became a hero back in Brazil and one of the victorious members of the Olympic men's beach volleyball team, Emanuel Rego, tried to present de Lima with his own gold medal as a substitute for the one he, perhaps, had lost so unfairly. De Lima refused. 'I cannot accept Emanuel's medal. I am happy with mine. It's bronze but it means gold,' he said.

As for Horan, he was fined and given a suspended prison sentence, but, perhaps an even greater shame, he subsequently appeared dancing an Irish jig on *Britain's Got Talent*.

Obviously, as rowers, we were less prone to outside interference, except by swans or low-flying kingfishers, but I do remember one occasion when I was rudely interrupted mid-race, and far from earning a Baron de Coubertin medal for sportsmanship I punched a hole in the canoe of two innocent girls.

I am not proud of this. It was the Royal Regatta at Henley in 1987. Andy Holmes and I had made the final of the coxless pairs against the famous Russian Pimenov brothers. Yuri and his twin Nikolay were the reigning world champions in the coxless pairs; Andy and I were world champions in the coxed

'I was scared, because I didn't know what could happen to me, whether he was armed with a knife, a revolver or something, and whether he was going to kill me.'
Vanderlei de Lima

pairs (with Pat Sweeney). We had never met before, so this was a serious showdown.

Two minutes into the race, we led by a length. At that point – and remember we're rowing backwards so we can't see what is up ahead – we slammed into a canoe containing two screaming girls. I was so angry, I punched a hole through the bottom of the boat.

The race was called to a halt and it was agreed we'd restart it from the beginning. We said we'd go for a 10-second warm-up before the start of the re-run to see if my hand was okay to row after punching the canoe. Unfortunately, the Pimenovs did not understand English too clearly and so when we started our warm-up, they thought the race was on again and shot off towards the finish. They had to be retrieved and headed back to the start. At the same point as the collision, in the re-run, we were the ones who were down in the race. You can imagine how we felt when we were leading comfortably at this point in the first run. We managed to draw ourselves level and ended up winning the race comfortably, by which time I was feeling very guilty about what I had done to that wooden canoe.

It turned out it wasn't the girls' fault at all. They wrote me a letter afterwards and explained what had happened. Some lads had pushed them off the bank without paddles and they had no method of getting out of our way. They felt as bad as I did. I have always wanted an old wooden Canadian canoe, and the only one I have seen up close I put my fist through!

There are times when the adrenalin that fires up competitiveness and the will-to-win makes you behave like an old bear with a sore head.

We managed to draw ourselves level and ended up winning the race comfortably, by which time I was feeling very guilty about what I had done to that wooden canoe.

Greg Louganis
Seoul 1988
Springboard diving

There are times when it all just goes horribly wrong. I am no stranger to that concept and neither was the great American diver, Greg Louganis, who arrived at my second Olympics in Seoul as an overwhelming favourite for two titles.

Four years previously in Los Angeles, at 24, he had already been regarded as one of the greatest divers there had ever been. He had not lost on platform or springboard for three years. The child of 15-year-old parents, of Samoan extraction, he had survived a traumatic childhood during which he had almost become a teenage alcoholic. Sport, as it so often does, had provided him with discipline, and a route out of trouble.

By Seoul, he had won 19 consecutive international springboard competitions between 1982 and 1987, although one Chinese rival, Tan Liangde, who, for six years, had been studying videotapes of Louganis in action, managed to pull off two sensational victories against the master in the lead-up to Seoul. Nevertheless, Louganis, the defending Olympic champion, was still considered supreme.

True to form, he was leading the preliminary round of the springboard competition when he stepped on to the board for this ninth dive, a reverse two-and-a-half somersault with pike. He leapt in the air, as he had done a thousand times, but on this occasion he failed to push out far enough. As he came down, his head crashed into the end of the board and he fell, with unaccustomed inelegance, into the water. Blood was seeping from the gash as he climbed out of the pool.

A mere 35 minutes later, he was back on the board with four temporary stitches in his head.

The next day he won his gold medal and went on, a week later, to earn a second gold in the platform event.

A mere 35 minutes later, he was back on the board with four temporary stitches in his head, and earned the highest score of any diver in the preliminaries with another reverse somersault. Only then was he taken to hospital for treatment and a waterproof patch. The next day he won his gold medal and went on, a week later, to earn a second gold in the platform event. Horrible accident though it was, for an athlete at the pinnacle of his sport, the show always goes on.

I knew Louganis slightly at these Olympics – unusually for me, because I was mostly suspended in a rowing-only bubble. He had taken a shine to one of the guys in the coxed four and used to turn up occasionally to have a chat with him.

It was only later, however, that Louganis confirmed he was gay and, indeed, HIV positive. It gave greater perspective on his reaction to winning his second gold medal, when he sobbed in the arms of his coach. Most people thought at the time it was just the natural reaction to his success. In fact, he had been contending with the huge stress of masking a potentially fatal condition. It may even have been as a result of this stress that he had suffered his accident in the first place.

At least that's something you can say for rowing. It's not life-threatening, as a rule. You pull muscles, you get miserable, you get cold, you ache, you eat too much, but there are no physically dangerous obstructions in your way. All my accidents, in a long and fairly torrid history, stemmed from off-the-field activities. As a teenager, I used to cut people's lawns for pocket money and succeeded in slicing a lump off my big toe through my trainers. Fellow Olympic rower, Ed Coode, once broke a bone in my foot while playing football.

Then there was the ill-conceived rugby match against a touring team, organised by another one of the GB rowers, Ben Hunt-Davis, when our coach, Jurgen, who would have forbidden such a thing, had gone home for Christmas. We rather fancied our chances, being egotistical sportsmen, and it was only during the match we discovered that two of their blokes played for Harlequins.

We should have sensed that the omens were bad when we discovered that all 15 players on our side had only ever been second-row forwards. I ended up at centre and within 10 minutes of the game I'd gone in for a tackle and not come out the other side. Instead, I was rolling on the floor in agony. I thought I'd broken my shoulder. In fact, I had ruptured the ligaments round the acromioclavicular joint at the top of the shoulder and had to admit as much, sheepishly, to Jurgen when he came back. He was not impressed; neither was he impressed the time I fell off a physio ball only months prior to Sydney and chipped a bone in my elbow.

The rider to the story is that I had reconstructive surgery to my shoulder when my rowing career was over. It seemed to be a success, but my consultant expressly forbade me to go skiing soon after the operation. I went skiing. I fell and, in considerable agony, thought I'd ruptured it again. Nine days later I went back, in both pain and trepidation, to see him and it turned out I'd only broken my collarbone. A lucky escape.

The conclusion you have to draw is that athletes, by nature, seem destined to push themselves into areas of risk. It probably isn't a coincidence that 10 years after Sydney both James Cracknell and I decided to cycle across America in different and unrelated events, and we both suffered unpleasant head injuries that truncated our experience.

As for Louganis, he went on to have an eclectic career which has included roles as an actor, dancer, dog trainer, speaker and Aids activist. But he will no doubt be best remembered for his wince-inducing moment on the springboard in Seoul.

The conclusion you have to draw is that athletes, by nature, seem destined to push themselves into areas of risk.

People at Marlow Rowing Club were telling me I was going to be an Olympic champion one day and I was only too happy to believe them.

Olympic Stadium
The first modern Olympics, Athens, 1896
Spyridon Louis
Athens 1896
Marathon

The Olympics changed my life. There is no doubt whatever about that. As a dyslexic, lazy comprehensive schoolboy, I would have had no more chance of becoming a public figure – I wouldn't have had the energy to rob a bank – than making it as an astronaut. I would probably have followed my dad into the building trade. I wasn't so bad at woodwork. It was my best GCSE result and, in my garage, I've still got the wooden cabinet I built – a bit rickety, but functional.

My dad always wanted me to carry on the family construction business, although he didn't tell me that. It was his private ambition, somewhat dampened when he took me to the building sites where he was working, to help him, only for me to stand around with my hands in my pockets and then scarper back to the river. He called me 'The Foreman' because I never actually did any work.

Well, that's not entirely true. I remember being on a site the day that John Lennon died in 1980 and I was working then, doing what I did (second) best – knocking things down.

But by then I'd discovered the thing I did better – rowing – and, as I say, it changed my life. In our first year as a school team, 1976, we entered seven events and won all seven. We instantly thought we were God's gift to the sport. By the time I was 17, people at Marlow Rowing Club were telling me I was going to be an Olympic champion one day and I was only too happy to believe them. It was just going to be a matter of time.

I missed the Moscow Olympics because of the boycott but, having set my sights on being a single sculler, I turned up at the senior World Championships convinced this would be the next stage in my inexorable climb to the top. It was probably the biggest lesson of my life. I was eliminated. I didn't even make the top 12.

And so I learned that nothing is inevitable. Making it to the top in sport entails hard work, preparation, belief, perseverance – not big muscles and big predictions. I always thought beforehand I'd do OK at Los Angeles, win in Seoul, and retire a satisfied gold medallist before the next Olympics, wherever they might be. Wrong. Our crew won gold, ahead of schedule, in Los Angeles. I was right about Seoul, winning a gold medal with Andy Holmes, and then came gold in Barcelona with Matt Pinsent, ditto in Atlanta and then a fifth gold medal with Matt, James Cracknell and Tim Foster in Sydney – ill, old, but finally, slightly, satisfied.

So much for predictions. I became, for want of a better word, famous. It was definitely not what I had sought from sport, being the shy, retiring type myself, but it came anyway and somehow you had to get on with it. To me, the purpose of sport wasn't fame, or money. For about 16 years I was more broke than anything else. Sport was freedom. As a non-academic with no brilliant professional future, sport was an escape, in my case to the river, where I could be good at something. Everything followed from that.

So I have some sympathy with Spyridon Louis, the 1896 marathon winner from Greece, who was elevated to hero status from humble origins for his achievement at the first modern Olympics. It is quite difficult to untangle the truth of his background from the multitude of legends that have grown up around him. Was he a shepherd, a soldier, a post-office messenger? Whatever he may have been, the story that he became inspired to run the marathon when he saw the stadium being erected in Athens is enshrined in Olympic history.

And so I learned that nothing is inevitable. Making it to the top in sport entails hard work, preparation, belief, perseverance – not big muscles and big predictions.

His preparation was purely comical. Forget long-term training and careful nutrition. He is said to have travelled with other competitors by horse-drawn cart to Marathon the day before the race, where they were all wined and dined by the mayor, which involved singing, eating and laughing until late into the evening. Anyone who knew me the day before a race would know that while eating was a definite priority, 'singing' and 'laughing' were not high on the agenda.

The next morning each runner was given two beers, at which point it begins to sound more like a pub crawl than a race. Eventually, the marathon began. Louis was running in shoes donated by his village. If we can believe the reports of the time, he was spurred on at the 14 kilometre mark by his stepfather presenting him with red wine and an Easter egg. I am beginning to like the sound of these arrangements.

As the race went on, his opposition fell by the wayside, perhaps in various shades of alcoholic stupor, and the man from Greece was declared the winner. He recalled the moment of victory in vivid fashion. 'Twigs and flowers were raining down on me. Everybody was calling my name and throwing their hats in the air. Afterwards it was printed in the papers that I asked for horses and a wagon as a reward … that is untrue.' Even then the media were misquoting.

He seemed a modest man, slightly baffled by the fuss. The shopkeepers of Athens tried to shower him with gifts, including watches, jewellery, wine, free haircuts, free clothing, free meals, a shotgun and a Singer sewing machine. Looking down that list, the only thing that really appeals to me is the meals.

It is said that as soon as he could Louis slipped back quietly to his village. There I identify with him completely. I have lived my whole life in Marlow, and have never sought nor wanted anything else.

> *His preparation was purely comical. Forget long-term training and careful nutrition.*

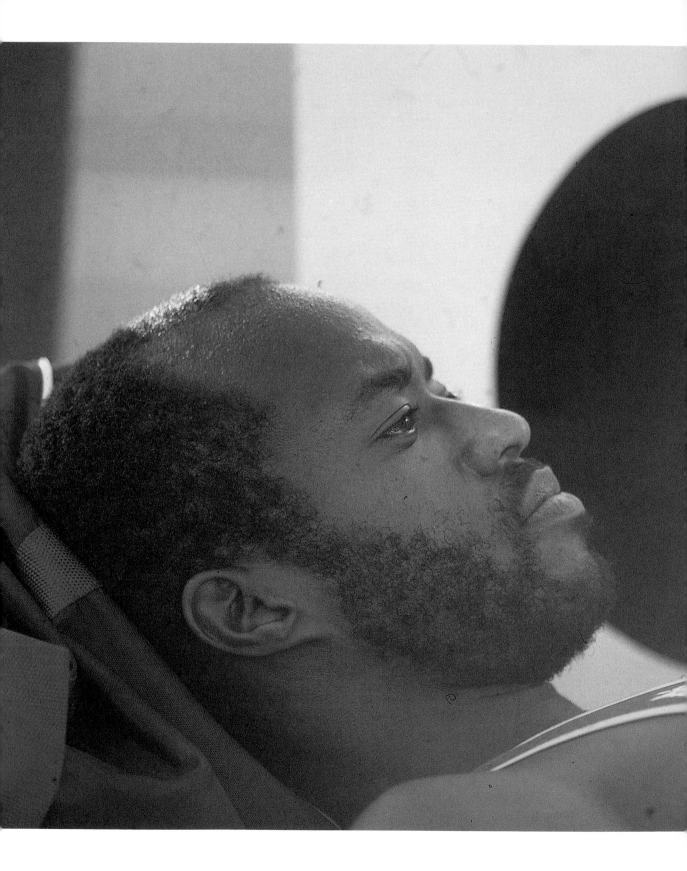

Edwin Moses
Los Angeles 1984
400 metres hurdles final

What do you think when you see this? Man relaxing on holiday? Dozing off using kitbag for pillow? Spacing out after a rather large lunch? In fact, it is a study of Edwin Moses, the world's greatest ever hurdler, about to compete in his most important race for eight years – the final of the 400 metres hurdles at the Los Angeles Olympics. This was his idea of preparation at the starting blocks. I don't often deal in superlatives, but this man was the near-perfect athlete.

For nine years, nine months and nine days he went undefeated. From 26 August 1977, when Harald Schmid of West Germany beat him in Berlin, to 4 June 1987, when his compatriot, Danny Harris, achieved the almost unimaginable feat of defeating him in Madrid, Moses won 122 consecutive races. They called him 'the bionic man', as though no mere mortal could achieve such consistency. I don't see that at all. I see a man who did all he could do to win. He was accused of masochistic workouts. Well, I'm bound to identify with that. 'Masochism' is a word that was applied to me. All it means is that I was prepared to work hard for what I wanted to be.

Moses was a science major at college. That helped. He studied physics and industrial engineering and, initially, had no intention of being an Olympic star, or an athlete of any kind. But when he was thrown off the football team for fighting – something I find quite interesting, given the zen-like character we came to see on the track – he discovered his nature was better suited to being an individual athlete. 'Everything is cut and dry. Nothing is arbitrary. It's just a matter of getting to the finish line first.'

There his views chime closely with mine. That is why I have very little patience with sports that are judged by arbitrary – sometimes biased, sometimes flat-out politically skewed – means. I have always held to the Olympic belief: 'May the fastest, strongest, best man win.'

Moses devastated the fields he raced against with a formidable amalgam of speed, sleekness, stamina, grace and, appropriately, technical engineering. A huge 9ft 9in stride gave him the ability to run 13 strides between hurdles, while his trailing rivals could manage a minimum of 14, and his improvement in the sport was so vast and so rapid that he won the first international event in which he competed – which happened to be the Montreal Olympics. He won by 8 metres, the largest winning margin in the history of the event.

By the time of the LA Olympic final, when he lay on the track, head resting on his kitbag, as though settling down for a good night's sleep, he had extended his winning streak to over 100 races, through 22 countries, including 89 finals. Here is one of my favourite statistics. By now, the 48 second barrier had been broken 32 times – once by John Akii-Bua of Uganda, once by Andre Phillips from the US, three times by Schmid and 27 times by Moses. It was not one of the shocks of the LA Games that he won the second gold medal of his career.

It is a measure of his dominance that even I, the one-track-minded rower competing in my first Olympics, should have taken time out of preoccupation-with-self to notice the greatness of Moses. I am sure that somewhere along the line I assimilated the way he worked and decided there was no other way.

I class him as one of the greatest athletes of our, of any, generation. But,

I class him as one of the greatest athletes of our, of any, generation. But, curiously, his aloofness, his ruthlessness, his very quietness, meant that he was not fully appreciated at the time.

curiously, his aloofness, his ruthlessness, his very quietness, meant that he was not fully appreciated at the time. There was no drama with Moses, merely relentless accomplishment. There was no personality on fulsome display, either. When they called him 'bionic man', it was less in praise than derision, as though he had eliminated the human frailties that make sport interesting to the masses.

I know I partially had that effect on people, too, but it was redeemed by the fact that I had celebrated health problems, which gave me an interesting sub-plot. Also I was surrounded by teammates who lifted me beyond the realm of 'boring' (well, partly) – James and his cockatoo hair colours, Tim punching through a glass window, Matt putting up with me for 10 years. Moses had no such devices. He was just an extremely competitive winner.

I hold the theory, rarely disproved, that athletes are often introverts. I've never met a greater example than Moses, as I know from first-hand experience. We met face-to-face for the first time in Atlanta in 1995 at a gathering on behalf of a charity. We were formally introduced by the chairman of the event, confident that we, as fellow athletes and mutual gold medallists, would have much in common. And we did. We shook hands and then just stood there looking at one another. No small talk. No talk at all. Two sporting introverts with nothing whatever to say to one another. There was a long, awkward silence, then someone must have intervened and spared us the head-on collision of two mutes. I think it's funny now. At the time I was just a bit baffled.

By now, the 48 sec barrier had been broken 32 times – once by John Akii-Bua of Uganda, once by Andre Phillips from the US, three times by Schmid and 27 times by Moses.

Opening Ceremony
Los Angeles 1984

It was my first Olympics, but there was no way I was going to the opening ceremony in Los Angeles. We had to go to bed at 7.15 every night to get into the routine we'd need for the rowing finals. We had to be up at 4.15 a.m. every day, and spending a late night with rocket men and balloons was not on the agenda.

But, believe it or not, I was sorry. This was the Olympics meets Hollywood. It had everything – eighty-four Kimball grand pianos, rocket-propelled men and, as you can see, large silver balls that even now remain inexplicable to me. It was a sign that times were changing. Notably, the 1976 Olympics in Montreal had been far less showy and ultimately less successful. Canadian tax payers lamented the expenditure for years.

LA changed all that. The Games were deemed a huge success. They made a profit. They made people, and countries, decide that the Olympics were worth bidding for after all. They had the 'Wow!' factor and razzmatazz – and, of course, I missed it.

I did go to the closing ceremony, which included an alien and a spaceman if I remember rightly. Pure kitsch. I loved it, but not enough to go to the opening ceremony in Seoul. Same reason. Andy Holmes and I were doubling up, i.e. entering the coxed and coxless pairs, and we had to save our energy for the rowing rather than take part in the opening celebrations. It was a sacrifice, but a minor one. Far, far better to be rested, relaxed and ready for your event than stay up half the night in a melee of athletes taking photos of the back of each other's heads.

That was the last time I had the luxury of saying no. Most athletes now are not given the choice!

This was the Olympics meets Hollywood. It had everything – grand pianos, rocket-propelled men and, as you can see, large silver balls.

123

In 1992 in Barcelona, as a two-time gold medallist, I was asked to carry the flag at the opening ceremony. I could have turned down the honour. We were staying in a village away from Barcelona and started racing a day and a half later, but our coach Jurgen Grobler said to me, 'It's a great honour for you, but also for the sport of rowing. We have to come up with a solution.' So I had to say yes.

Another problem was Matthew, or more specifically, one of Matthew's dares. We both remembered a Russian weightlifter who carried the Soviet flag at the Moscow Games with one hand, and now Matthew was daring me to do the same thing. If so much as a sniff of this had reached Jurgen, he'd have banned it straightaway (wrists are quite important to rowers), so we had to make sure he didn't hear a whisper.

I was torn about what to do until the very last minute, but when the flag was put into my right hand, that's where it stayed, alone.

I thought I'd get my revenge on Matthew at Atlanta. The sport of rowing was asked to provide the flag carrier again and we all just assumed this meant Matthew. It didn't. It meant me, in a deviation from Olympic history. No Briton has ever carried the flag twice before. So, obviously, this time I had to carry it in my left hand alone. This is the trouble with athletes. You are always in a state of escalation.

LA changed all that. The Games were deemed a huge success. They made a profit. They made people, and countries, decide that the Olympics were worth bidding for after all. They had the 'Wow!' factor and razzmatazz – and, of course, I missed it.

But it wasn't the flag that caused the most amusement this time. It was the chaos. The British chef de mission at the time was Simon Clegg, who, because of his military background, took great pains to make sure we would conduct ourselves with decorum and precision as we entered the Olympic Stadium and marched round the track at the opening ceremony. He was a stickler for instructions, these being that we would file out of the holding area and walk two-by-two like animals into the ark, smallest at front, largest at rear, upright and smart, into the stadium.

I definitely remember Greg Searle leading a chant of 'Stevo, Stevo' like a bunch of football fans as they clustered around me.

That was fine, but, looking at the television screens available to us, we could see that the athletes from other countries were entering the stadium at high speed, six or eight at a time. You didn't need a degree in maths to work out that these two sets of circumstances didn't quite add up.

Sure enough, we marched out of the holding area to be greeted by officials shouting, 'Go – go – GO!' as a yawning gap had opened up ahead. So much for smallest at front. They were trampled out of the way by the hulking rowing team, among others, who caught up with me jogging with the flag. I definitely remember Greg Searle leading a chant of 'Stevo, Stevo' like a bunch of football fans as they clustered around me and charged into the arena with all the smart precision of a herd of rhinos. The whole thing was a chaotic mess. Poor Simon, but good fun.

Sydney? Luckily, less madness to report. Matt carried the flag this time – yes, one-handed. The only downside was the slightly silly outfits we all had to wear. Sailor suits are the words that spring to mind, and they are not good words, either. I gritted my teeth and got on with it. Matt did no such thing. He had his trousers tailored so that the bell bottoms didn't flap like one of Ben Ainslie's sails in the wind. I took the view, as I so often do, that I couldn't be bothered.

Harold Osborn
Paris 1924
High jump

Dick Fosbury
Mexico 1968
High jump

All it took was one clever scientific mind to see where the human race was going wrong. No disrespect to Harold Osborn, who won the Olympic high jump in 1924 with success at the record height of 6ft 6in – that's jumping over me – but when you look at the black-and-white pictures of the old technique, it seems almost ridiculously old-fashioned. And look what the competitors are landing on – flattened sand. What a prospect – win a gold medal, break your arm!

That's not to say that Dick Fosbury's way, unveiled 44 years later, had no injury potential. The minor disadvantage of the high-jump technique that we have all come to know as the 'Fosbury Flop' was that you landed on the back of your neck.

This is fine now we have foam landing pits, but when, as a university student, Fosbury was trying out the new idea, health and safety requirements hadn't progressed beyond a bucket of sand. But he remained undaunted. With a study background in physics and engineering, the American had concluded that

Look what the competitors are landing on – flattened sand. What a prospect – win a gold medal, break your arm!

rather than attempt to clear the bar by the customary 'straddle' or the 'western roll' – when the whole body was more or less horizontal above the bar – there was, ergonomically, a better way.

He deduced it was better to clear the bar backwards, rolling in an arc, with the head and feet vertically below the hips at the peak of the arc on opposite sides of the bar. Don't ask me how he thought of that. I don't remember my physics lessons going that well at school; or me going to the lessons at all, come to think of it. I had urgent business on the river bank.

It was good enough that Fosbury understood what he was doing. He worked out that by operating along this rolling arc, it was possible for the jumper to keep the body's centre of gravity below, rather than above, the height of the bar. Even I can see that's a good thing.

The Olympic final in Mexico proved it. The contest was reduced to a three-way challenge between himself, Ed Caruthers of the US and Valentin Gavrilov of the Soviet Union. The height of the bar was raised to 7ft 4¼in, a new Olympic record. Gavrilov and Caruthers failed three times. Fosbury failed twice, but at the last attempt succeeded and changed sporting life as we knew it. By 1980, 13 of the 16 Olympic finalists were using the Fosbury Flop.

I never really had the body for high jumping myself. I did do it at school (scissor-kick style – they probably didn't trust us not to get concussed using the Fosbury Flop) but I preferred shot put, discus, long jump and sprinting. For some reason, I couldn't throw the javelin to save my live. It flopped rather than flew.

As for team sports, I played a bit of rugby because I was fast and big, and I have memories of being the school football team reserve goalkeeper – not good memories, either. We must have had a good team because I wasn't called into action very much. This left me feeling rather bored, so to pass the time I jumped up and down, just touching (I swear) the crossbar. Unfortunately, it broke in half and I stood there holding it, wondering what to do. The sports master was so furious he came bounding up, snatched the bar out of my hand and brought down the goalpost as well. I didn't laugh (until later).

The minor disadvantage of the high-jump technique that we have all come to know as the 'Fosbury Flop' was that you landed on the back of your neck.

Jesse Owens
Berlin 1936
Triple sprint and long jump champion

One of the greatest athletes of all time, Jesse Owens was born almost a century ago, and the pictures that have been passed down to us are, appropriately, in black and white. That sums up the story of Jesse Owens – discrimination against black people and the theory of white supremacy. One young athlete from Cleveland, Alabama, the grandson of slaves, the youngest of 10, upstaged and subverted the entire Nazi propaganda machine by winning four gold medals to establish one simple fact. He was faster, stronger, better than anyone else in the field. Hitler's twisted philosophy was exposed in the time it took for Owens to win the 100 yard dash, 10.3 seconds. He went on to win the 200 metres, the 4 x 100 relay and the long jump, and it is the long-jump competition that I find so interesting.

Intriguingly, perhaps even dangerously, he struck up a friendship with his German rival, Luz Long. Here they are, a moment captured at the Berlin Olympics, and the body language suggests a genuine closeness. What Hitler made of this unlikely event you can only imagine, but it cannot have been good for Luz's long-term health. But even without that extra political dimension, friendships between rivals are rare enough.

I can't remember ever having sat down with an opponent in such a friendly way during an Olympics, or during my life, for that matter. Basically, I have never made a friend of a rival. I wouldn't ignore them. I didn't want to give them a better reason to beat me than just being a favourite for the gold. But as for chatting to them, getting on with them, sharing tactical thoughts, the whole thing is unimaginable.

I am not really a sociable person. I didn't enter sport looking for friends. I have always been shy. I was uncomfortable – still

But since when was sport about human decency? I can only imagine that Long believed he could win the gold medal and wanted to do so against the best possible opposition. I understand that.

am – in large groups of people. Of course, there was camaraderie in rowing, especially with my teammates and fellow gold medallists in Sydney. I always had a close relationship with Matt Pinsent. Tim Foster was the easiest person to get along with, although he keeps himself to himself, and I think, with James Cracknell, I was more like a father figure than a contemporary because of the 10 year age gap.

My best friend always was, and probably always will be, 'Bill' Haley. It wasn't his real name. Robert was his proper name, but you know what school kids are like. Bill Haley, the rock'n'roll singer from the fifties, was still pretty popular when I was at school, so we overruled his parents and gave him the nickname, which stuck.

It suited him. He was fun. We rowed together. Our big plan had been to compete in the 1979 World Championships in Moscow, but a rogue seat in our boat had wrecked that dream. I always imagined that Bill and I would go through life together, getting into scrapes and getting out of them again, living in and out of each other's houses, me the quiet one, him the extrovert. I really looked up to him.

But unknown to us, and to him, he had a heart condition. He was round at my house one day when he collapsed and died right in front of my eyes. I never had such a close friend again. I don't know whether there is a deep, psychological reason for that – something about not wanting to lose someone again in such traumatic circumstances – or whether I'm just anti-social.

I was such a quiet person, who wouldn't say boo to a goose. Bill was the opposite. So friendship between opposites appeals to me. Owens and Long, black and white, American and German, direct opponents, one scorned in his own country, the other revered – the fact that they warmed to each other was extraordinary to say the least. They can scarcely have known each other for more than a few days, but the impression on the American was profound. He wrote later: 'What I remember most was the friendship I struck up with Luz Long, the German long jumper. He was my strongest rival, yet it was he who advised me to adjust my run-up in the qualifying round and thereby helped me to win. Our friendship was important to me. We corresponded regularly until Hitler invaded Poland and then the letters stopped.'

You've got to say, if the story is exactly as Owens reported, that for Long to advise his most dangerous opponent to move back his run-up a yard to help ensure qualification for the final is a heart-warming tale of human decency.

But since when was sport about human decency? I can only imagine that Long believed he could win the gold medal and wanted to do so against the best possible opposition. I understand that. To win is good, but to win against minor opposition saps the full satisfaction of the moment. Would I have done it? Modern professionalism would probably have prevented me, just as cricketers don't walk when they're out, footballers dive, and every cheap little advantage is sought in the quest for victory. In contrast, the tradition of fair play is still upheld in some sports. Golfers and snooker players will call strokes and penalties on themselves.

Owens promptly out-jumped Long to the gold medal, but Long's advice had been a fine and generous act on a human level, one that defied the twisted code of Nazi supremacy. It cannot have been easy, nor entirely safe, to deny the prejudice that Hitler held so dear. Long was a decent and, beyond that, brave Olympian. So much was recognised many years later when he was posthumously awarded the Baron de Coubertin medal for sportsmanship.

As Owens said, they corresponded following Berlin, but the letters from Long suddenly stopped. He was called up to fight and was killed by Allied action in Italy in 1943. He was only 30 years old. But Owens persisted with the connection and continued a correspondence with his friend's son until his own death in 1980.

It cannot have been easy, nor entirely safe, to deny the prejudice that Hitler held so dear.

Dorando Pietri

London 1908
Marathon

One of the most dramatic moments in Olympic history is depicted here – the 1908 marathon. The fourth modern Games were slightly thrown together due to the eruption of Mount Vesuvius in Italy. They had originally been scheduled for Rome but were re-routed to London, which allocated the grand total of £15,000 to stage them. White City was to be the hub of the enterprise, and the marathon – a 25 mile run in honour of the mythical Pheidippides – was set to finish in the magnificent new stadium.

But royalty was not amused. Queen Victoria's granddaughter, Princess Mary, wanted to watch the start of the race from the nursery window at Windsor Castle, so would the organisers please add just a mile to the distance. It wasn't a question, either. And then Queen Victoria's daughter-in-law, Princess Alexandra, made it known that she would rather like to see the finish under the royal box. So another 385 yards were added.

I had no idea when I ran my marathon that I was suffering an extra one mile, 385 yards on a royal whim. I might have had a word at my knighthood if I'd known.

I had no idea when I ran my marathon that I was suffering an extra one mile, 385 yards on a royal whim. I might have had a word at my knighthood if I'd known.

There was tremendous interest in the marathon. The day dawned hot and muggy and thousands of spectators lined the route. The difficult conditions made for an eventful race, but two runners separated themselves from the rest of the pack and it appeared the gold medal would be decided between them.

Charles Hefferon of South Africa led by three minutes at the 18 mile mark over the little Italian Dorando Pietri, but two miles later the second man began to close the gap. In this he was helped by the fact that Hefferon had accepted a glass of champagne *en route*, which caused him stomach cramps and dizziness. Meanwhile, three Americans, led by Johnny Hayes, were beginning to gain on the leading pair.

It was Pietri who entered the stadium first, but it became immediately clear that all was not well. Such was his state of dehydraton and exhaustion, he seemed dazed and began to stumble in the wrong direction. Officials redirected him, but then he collapsed on to the track. Typically, the British crowd, with a suffering underdog auditioning before their very eyes, instantly took up his cause. They screamed for people

Typically, the British crowd, with a suffering underdog auditioning before their very eyes, instantly took up his cause.

to help him, while the more knowing in the audience screamed as loudly for people to leave him alone. They knew that if physical aid was given to any competitor, he would be disqualified.

It was agony to watch. Each time he struggled to his feet, he would plod a few steps before collapsing again, and all the time, Hayes was gaining ground just outside the stadium.

In the end, it was too much for one of the British officials. When Pietri started to collapse again, for the fifth time, just short of the finish line, Jack Andrew, the head organiser of the race, caught him and carried him bodily over the line. In the words of the official report, released later: 'It was impossible to leave him there, for it looked as if he might die in the very presence of the Queen.' How very inconvenient of him.

Of course, the Americans filed an immediate protest and quite rightly the race was awarded to Hayes, who finished in an Olympic record time of 2 hours 55 minutes 18 seconds. But in the eyes of the world it was Pietri who emerged a hero. He became an instant celebrity and, by way of apology for his sufferings (and, she might have added, that crucial extra mile-and-a-bit) the Queen awarded him a special gold cup the next day.

His sensational and agonising effort sparked a marathon craze around the globe that had unfortunately not expired by the time I made my debut in London in 2003. Luckily, we knew more about hydration by then. My only fear was being overtaken by a rhino.

> *Each time he struggled to his feet, he would plod a few steps before collapsing again, and all the time, Hayes was gaining ground just outside the stadium.*

Paula Radcliffe

Athens 2004
Marathon

Paula Radcliffe won the London Marathon in 2003 in a scarcely believable world-record time of 2 hours, 15 minutes, 25 seconds. I had to believe it, because I was standing there at the time. If you look at old photos of her crossing the line, one of the hands holding the finishing tape belonged to me.

By then, I was a marathon veteran myself. I'd run the distance in 2001, to help raise money for my charities, in a time that was not a world record. It was virtually double Paula's future world mark – 4 hours 20 minutes, if anyone needs to know. It was a great day, though, and I enjoyed the atmosphere, especially wearing bib No. 1, although when the running started, I can confidently say that never has bib No. 1 receded so fast through the field. I was overtaken by Elvis Presleys, caterpillars, old men. The only thing I can say with a degree of pride was that I did beat all the rhinos. Eventually, Ann and I crossed the finish line together, and, aside from the pain, it gave us both a feeling of immense accomplishment.

So I knew something about the marathon at the Athens Olympics, where Paula was the favourite and widely perceived as Britain's greatest opportunity for an athletics medal. But that, as it transpired, was crazy. How can a country so obsessed by the weather have been so heedless of its potential effect?

In homage to the founding of the ancient Olympics, the marathon was beginning at Marathon, and it so happened that I was travelling down that very road on the morning of the race. It was the middle Sunday of the Games and I'd been out at the rowing lake, my first experience of commentating on an Olympics instead of competing in them. We were driving along in a comfortably air-conditioned car, but the heat was

> *How can a country so obsessed by the weather have been so heedless of its potential effect?*

so intense outside the windscreen it was almost tangible. You could see it shimmering off the tarmac. It was so hot the road looked as though it was melting, and I pitied those poor girls having to run in such conditions.

More to the point, I pitied the pale-skinned blonde, who would be running for Britain in dangerous heat, alien to her preferred conditions. She was at such a distinct disadvantage and it was completely out of her control.

So the unfolding of the trauma that day in Athens was partially not her fault. With the sun burning down and the leaders of the race now beyond her reach, she pulled out of the marathon at the 22 mile mark, sitting, sobbing, on the kerb at the side of the road until she was comforted by old friends and retrieved by race officials. Her devastation was portrayed in two ways by the British media. They love this type of thing. Failure is one of the great staples of the press. Some offered sympathy, others accused her of quitting and really turned the knife.

Sometimes I think sport is hard enough as it is, without those who comment on it then crucifying the victims. I speak as one who has had a good ride from the British media, but then I didn't fail at the Olympics.

The only thing of which I would be constructively critical was her preparation. She didn't join the rest of the British training camp in Cyprus. Instead, she chose to take herself off to somewhere in Seville, where the conditions were too hot and the ground unsuitable. Many of the roads had cracked and dried out, and she suffered a leg injury. That led to her intake of strong anti-inflammatories, which she claimed prevented her from absorbing nutrients from her food adequately. All these things may have affected her negatively before the race, but I still believe the heat was the most telling issue on the day.

I remember the fierce debate afterwards. Should she or shouldn't she run in the 10,000 metres? Most people decided no. The risk of a second failure was too great. It wasn't her

The heat was so intense outside the windscreen it was almost tangible. You could see it shimmering off the tarmac. It was so hot the road looked as though it was melting.

favoured distance. It was only five days after the marathon. But she entered and I didn't blame her. I would have run, too, if I'd been her.

It was one of Ann's worst nightmares. For years, my wife has been the rowing team doctor, as she was in Sydney, and her greatest fear was having one day to tell me – diabetic, suffering from colitis, taking medication – that I was unfit to row. She knew that there was no one as pig-headed, as never-say-never, as I am. I think I would have rowed anyway. Fortunately, it never came to that. I was not fully fit in Sydney, I hadn't been for years, but I rowed. I felt terrible, but we won and I got over it. It was worth it.

So I understand Paula. Rationally, it was never going to work, and it didn't. She pulled out of the race with eight laps remaining, just stepping off the track, no tears this time. But I think, good or bad, it gave her closure. She had done her best. She didn't have to spend the rest of her life thinking 'what if'.

There is a footnote to my personal marathon story. Ann and I stayed overnight in the Tower Hotel after the 2001 race, along with all the other athletes and VIPs. I came down to breakfast the next morning with horribly stiff muscles, barely able to walk. It was depressing. That's what comes of age and decrepitude I thought. Then I saw the men's winner come in, Abdelkader El Mouaziz of Morocco, and to my great delight he was hobbling, too.

'And he had it easy,' I told myself smugly. 'He was only on the course for two hours or so. I was out there for twice that!'

Failure is one of the great staples of the press. Some offered sympathy, others accused her of quitting and really turned the knife.

141

Steve Redgrave
Sydney 2000
Coxless men's four

It's Tim I felt sorry for. This was the ultimate day for me, my ultimate moment, winning my fifth Olympic gold medal. But for Tim Foster, one of my crew mates that day in Sydney, it may have been a slightly less clear-cut celebratory occasion. When I look back at this photograph, it is not the sheer pain and exhaustion I mainly remember, because that was the same after every race. Peculiarly enough, I think of Tim, and laugh.

It all began for him many years before, when he and Matt Pinsent were starting out as world-class rowers together. This was before Matt hooked up with me as a partner. They were more than promising. They won gold at the junior World Championships in 1988, the same year that Andy Holmes and I won Olympic gold in Seoul. But, as so often happens in sport, fate took them in entirely separate directions.

Matt's career sailed upwards. He joined up with me and we won gold at Barcelona and then Atlanta in the coxless pairs. Tim, however, had a tougher time. His progress stalled. Even

This was the ultimate day for me, my ultimate moment, winning my fifth Olympic gold medal. But for Tim Foster, one of my crew mates that day in Sydney, it may have been a slightly less clear-cut celebratory occasion.

143

when he joined Matt, James Cracknell and I in the coxless four bound for Sydney, he didn't enjoy a straightforward run. First, he stuck his hand through a window at a party and had to fight his way back into the boat after an injury layoff. Then he developed a seriously bad back, which had him lying flat out, entire career threatened, in the run-up to the 2000 Games. It was always touch-and-go for him.

He must have dreamed every night about the feel of a gold medal round his neck after all his setbacks and disappointments. And here you see it. In that golden moment of triumph, Matt stumbles back in his elation to hug me, and the first thing Tim gets around his neck is Matt's groin. That's why I laugh.

I suppose some people might think this is a rather irreverent way of looking back on the greatest sporting instant of my life, but I have never been a romantic about sport. I was always a pragmatist. Hard work = result. You can't escape that single fact, unless you're tanked up on drugs, which I wasn't prepared to do.

Even in the horrendous hour before our race in Sydney, when my mind was in turmoil and I was wishing I was a thousand miles away, actually 10,000 miles away, I was still a pragmatist at heart. I had been told by my doctors that they had no idea how my body would respond to the six-and-a-half minutes of unparalleled effort I was about to put in, and I might perhaps fall into a coma because of the sudden drop in blood sugar levels.

I had been told by my doctors that they had no idea how my body would respond to the six-and-a-half minutes of unparalleled effort I was about to put in, and I might perhaps fall into a coma because of the sudden drop in blood sugar levels.

I have never been a romantic about sport. I was always a pragmatist. Hard work = result. You can't escape that single fact, unless you're tanked up on drugs, which I wasn't prepared to do.

None of this dissuaded me in the least, but I did go into the makeshift canteen at the rowing lake just before we were due to climb into the boat and help myself to a packet of sugar. I reasoned that if I felt myself fainting during the warm-up, I could grab the sugar and swallow it. I had been through this routine many times, but not under the pressure of the Olympic finals. I sellotaped the packet to the bottom of the boat and then forgot all about it. Didn't need it, didn't faint, did win.

It was only much later, when I saw our boat on display at the Henley River and Rowing Museum, still with the packet of sugar taped to the bottom, that I was reminded of it. I suppose I should have mentioned it to someone, have them save it for posterity, as proof of my madness, maybe, because next time I went it was gone. Some tidy-minded cleaner must have gone in and thought: 'What's that doing there?' Anyway, someone had ripped it off and binned it.

It's hard to believe that over a decade has gone by since that moment. Rowing was my life for so long, with all the dreaded training that went with it. Twenty years in a boat, going backwards – I'm not sure how much that

counts as a human achievement, especially as much of it was conducted in poverty and reliance on my long-suffering wife, Ann, to run the home and family as well as establish her own practice as a doctor and osteopath.

I'd come a long way, all the way from losing a beautiful baby competition at Butlin's – my mum, Sheila, would have disputed that result – to winning five Olympic gold medals. And that's where, I suppose, I wouldn't knock myself. I had an opportunity to win once every four years, for five Olympic cycles. When I had to, I did.

But I didn't do it alone and remain thankful to my coaches Francis Smith, Mike Spracklin and Jurgen Grobler, as well as all my Olympic rowing mates down the years – Andy Holmes, Martin Cross, Adrian Ellison, Richard Budgett, Pat Sweeney, Matt, James and Tim.

Andy tragically died at the age of 51 after contracting Weil's disease following a sculling marathon. It was a random and terrible thing to happen, and something that any of us could have suffered during a life on the river, since it is a waterborne disease, carried by rats. We'd seen each other at Henley Regatta recently, after a long gap of years, and he was talking enthusiastically about coming back to rowing. I was

My pass in woodwork remained my main claim to fame at school, until, that is, Mr Smith took a few of us likely lads down to the Thames and introduced us to the sport of rowing. Without that single event – and I only went to get out of schoolwork – my life would have been different indeed.

Somewhere in a drawer are five Olympic gold medals and they tell me that, with a great deal of help and support, and along with my crew mates, once upon a time I achieved something else. I did my best. What more is there than that?

delighted about that. We arranged to see each other again. I couldn't believe it when I heard the news. I was so sorry for his family. He became a father for the fifth time just a month before he died.

It reminds you, dramatically, that you never know what will happen next. I didn't. I thought vaguely I'd be working in my dad's construction business one day, since I showed no academic aptitude at all. My pass in woodwork remained my main claim to fame at school, until, that is, Mr Smith took a few of us likely lads down to the Thames and introduced us to the sport of rowing. Without that single event – and I only went to get out of schoolwork – my life would have been different indeed.

That's why I have been such a passionate supporter of widening the availability of sport to every child in the country. I hope London 2012 changes the way we see sport, so it is not an optional extra for children, but a genuine, integral part of their lives, because it can lead to undreamed of achievement.

Sometimes I think my greatest achievement these days is playing two sets of squash, which is not bad for an old boy. But somewhere in a drawer are five Olympic gold medals and they tell me that, with a great deal of help and support, and along with my crew mates, once upon a time I achieved something else. I did my best. What more is there than that?

Tommie Smith, John Carlos and Peter Norman: the Black Power Salute

Mexico 1968
200 metres award ceremony

It is always the incidental things in a story that get you. Peter Norman. Who was he? The *other* man on the podium, second in the race, witness and bystander to the most famous, non-violent protest in the history of the Olympic Games. Except it turns out that he wasn't a mere bystander after all.

I was six when it happened, so not fully genned up on racial politics, and it was years before I understood that Norman was, in fact, a full participant at the event, which so scandalised the Olympic authorities they threatened to throw out the entire US track and field team.

Before the race was run, Norman, the young Australian and Salvation Army officer, had discussed the protest with the two black athletes, who were determined to make their mark on the Games. When – and this is my favourite detail – Carlos remembered he'd forgotten his black gloves, it was Norman who suggested that the protesters wear one of Smith's gloves each. So that iconic picture, one gloved fist raised in symbolic defiance against anti-black discrimination, was partly the result of a memory lapse and an Aussie's suggestion.

It was none the less powerful for that, and it caused huge offence and outrage at the time among those who were part of the predominantly white establishment. One American

It caused huge offence and outrage at the time among those who were part of the predominantly white establishment.

149

commentator described Smith and Carlos as 'black-skinned stormtroopers'. It's language from another century, another world, but still shocking to see in print.

The IOC insisted that both men (perhaps they were unaware of Norman's collusion or perhaps he was protected by the colour of his skin) were to be banned from further Olympic competition, by which they meant the team relays. The US team officials initially refused, but ultimately capitulated when the dire threat to throw out the whole US track and field team was held over them.

Not everyone was horrified. Even as the fury raged, the Australian chef de mission, Julius 'Judy' Patching, resisted calls from the country's conservative media for Norman to be punished, and took a rather more relaxed view of the affair. This sounds typically Australian to me, and even if it didn't happen, you like to think it did. He apparently told Norman at the time, 'They're screaming out for your blood, so consider yourself severely reprimanded. Now, you got any tickets for the hockey today?'

Everything about the Norman story is intriguing – his late gutsy run to secure the silver, his one-man, one-glove inspiration, his simple insistence after the race that 'I believe that every man is born equal and should be treated that way.' He showed great courage in his solidarity with the black cause.

Meanwhile, Smith and Carlos had been treated like pariahs. The doors of America clanged shut on them. They found it incredibly difficult to find work. Both their marriages disintegrated.

What happened next? Norman continued running until 1985, when an Achilles tendon injury became infected, and gangrene set in. He avoided amputation only because one doctor argued with his colleagues that 'you can't cut off the leg of an Olympic silver medallist'.

Meanwhile, Smith and Carlos had been treated like pariahs. The doors of America clanged shut on them. They found it incredibly difficult to find work. Both their marriages disintegrated with Carlos's wife committing suicide.

Slowly, over time, they were rehabilitated, not because they surrendered their beliefs but because white establishment America apparently surrendered its own prejudices. In 2005, Norman met Smith and Carlos for the last time when San Jose State University, California, unveiled a statue, based on the photo, of its two former students. With typical modesty, Norman downplayed his role. 'People don't realise that they sacrificed their lives for a cause they believed in, and it was peaceful and non-violent,' he said. 'I was glad I was with them.'

After Norman died suddenly the following year, both black athletes spoke proudly of their friend. Smith called him 'a man of solid beliefs, a humanitarian'. Carlos, to whom Norman was closer, said simply, 'Peter Norman was my brother.'

Both black athletes spoke proudly of their friend. Smith called him 'a man of solid beliefs, a humanitarian'. Carlos, to whom Norman was closer, said simply, 'Peter Norman was my brother.'

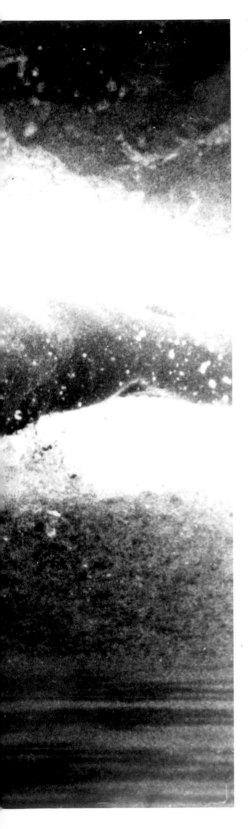

Mark Spitz
Munich 1972
Swimming

What I love about this picture is you can see how much it hurts. There is no holding back. Usually swimming looks smooth and almost effortless (unless I'm doing it), as apparently weightless bodies power up and down the pool. But even if he's only trying to keep the chlorine out of his eyes, I think the competitive demons that drove American swimmer Mark Spitz to his seven Olympic gold medals in Munich betray themselves in the image.

Spitz made a tremendous impression on me at the time. I was 10 years old and avidly watching the Olympics on television. I remember being sent out to collect the newspapers and milk from the bottom of our drive at home, and my eye being caught by the *Daily Mirror* headline as I carried it back to the house. 'SPITZ FOR SIX' was splattered all over the back page. He wanted to be the first athlete in any sport to win six gold medals in one Olympic Games, and the idea completely captured my imagination – this guy, day after day, getting more and more gold medals. I was inspired by the thought: 'Wouldn't it be great to win one!'

Spitz made a tremendous impression on me at the time. I was 10 years old and avidly watching the Olympics on television.

He went one better in the end. He won seven, and he broke the world record in the process every time.

I met Mark many years later. We were on a roof somewhere in Athens, along with Carl Lewis, being interviewed by the BBC about the Olympics in progress. Here was my opportunity to thank the man who, you could argue, had planted the idea of becoming an Olympic champion in my head. I didn't. I don't think either of them knew who I was. They were nice enough, but I certainly had the impression they felt they were bigger stars, and in some ways they were right. Swimming and athletics are so much more noticeable than rowing as Olympic sports. I didn't mind.

But then swimmers, and athletes to some extent, have so many golds to shoot for at any one Olympic Games that I think it can devalue them. The media came after me when Michael Phelps broke Spitz's record, winning eight golds in Beijing. I avoided them. I didn't want to say what I was thinking. Fortunately, Michael Johnson said it for me. He said that in athletics it was possible to win more than one medal, but they don't give them out 'for going backwards and sideways'.

He wanted to be the first athlete in any sport to win six gold medals in one Olympic Games, and the idea completely captured my imagination — this guy, day after day, getting more and more gold medals. I was inspired by the thought: 'Wouldn't it be great to win one!'

It is too possible to win a glut of medals in swimming, and that is what lowers their value in my eyes.

Do I think Phelps is the greatest Olympic athlete ever? His gold tally (14 in two Games) says yes he is. In fact, if he were a country, he'd be about 15th in the all-time medal-winning table. But, in my view, the answer is no. It is too possible to win a glut of medals in swimming, and that is what lowers their value in my eyes.

It didn't surprise me that Spitz didn't go to watch Michael Phelps beat his record in Beijing. He said it was because he hadn't been invited. 'I'm going to sit there and watch Michael Phelps break my record anonymously? That's almost demeaning to me. It is not almost – it is.'

I think, having played golf with him in a 'celebrity' version of the Ryder Cup (Europe v USA) in 2005, that he couldn't bear to go. All athletes are competitive, but some are more competitive than others. I would know. I'm probably one of them. I'm just quieter about it than Spitz ever was.

Ingemar Stenmark

Lake Placid 1980
Slalom skiing

Skiing has been one of the great pleasures of my life, along with golf (on good days), training (on good days) and winning at absolutely anything.

Between skiing and bobsledding, I have had my fair share of action in the snow, but I would never dream of calling myself a skilled skier. I like travelling fast on skis. Far from demonstrating finesse, I'm more like a solid boulder that gathers speed. Falling is an occupational hazard, and I have the broken bones to prove it.

In terms of ability, I share absolutely nothing with one of the most supreme and powerful slalom racers in the history of the sport, Ingemar Stenmark, who was a double gold medallist at Lake Placid in 1980. He had arrived at the Olympics as the overwhelming favourite, having 14 consecutive giant-slalom wins behind him, and yet he was a little overwhelmed himself. A year earlier, he had suffered a bad fall and serious concussion, and the mental scars seemed to be lingering. He admitted later that he arrived at Lake Placid in a dangerously cautious state of mind.

In terms of ability, I share absolutely nothing with one of the most supreme and powerful slalom racers in the history of the sport.

He was an introvert anyway, supporting my general theory that while extroverts go into the theatre, shy characters cope best with the sometimes soulless loneliness of training.

Stenmark, born in Lapland, grew up in the isolated, wind-chilled mountains of Sweden, 700km (435 miles) north of Stockholm. Naturally, his pastime was skiing. A shy and withdrawn boy, he said, 'I skied because I could do it alone.'

By the time he was 20, he was the supreme slalom and giant-slalom performer in the world, and some people no doubt thought his acquisition of the gold medals in Lake Placid was a mere formality. But sport is no blind follower of the form book.

Stenmark himself was nervous. Following the first run of the giant slalom (there were two runs to decide the medal), he was lying in third place, having skied to minimise risk. He was sadly frustrated with himself. 'If I had ended up number two behind Andreas Wenzel of Liechtenstein, it would still have been a good result. But I would have been really, really disappointed.'

Prior to the second and deciding run, he was even more worried. 'Fifteen minutes before the race I was so nervous that my legs felt wobbly. Then, when I started, I felt nothing of that.'

Every athlete on earth probably shares the same feelings. The nerves just stop when the race begins. You're so familiar with everything you do, every muscle movement has been made a thousand times before, you just seem to slide into something close to routine. Maybe I was just completely committed to what I had to do next, but I can't ever remember feeling remotely scared once the hooter to start a race had sounded. In mortal pain, yes, but never scared.

Stenmark seemed to experience the same thing. He went up the mountain a worried man, and came down again the champion. He went on to complete the slalom double at those Olympics and he remains, partly because of the sheer difficulty

'If I could start again, I wouldn't have become a slalom skier. I would have gone for a team sport. Then you don't have to be the best all the time to enjoy it and the team can be good even if you have a bad day. You can share everything with others, success as well as failure. I think it's nicer to compete in a team sport.'

Ingemar Stenmark

of his sport, one of my favourite athletes. It is extraordinary to think that he could slide and turn between gates faster than I can ski flat out downhill. It's slightly depressing to think that, too.

Interestingly, for such a loner by nature, he was never entirely happy with being an individual sportsman. He once said, 'If I could start again, I wouldn't have become a slalom skier. I would have gone for a team sport. Then you don't have to be the best all the time to enjoy it and the team can be good even if you have a bad day. You can share everything with others, success as well as failure. I think it's nicer to compete in a team sport.'

So there's conclusive proof that we never get everything we want. I have always regretted that I didn't make it as a single sculler. Stenmark, undeniably the best slalom skier of all time, regretted he didn't make it in the Swedish Davis Cup team. Maybe athletes are never satisfied. It's the competitor in us. We even compete with our own fate.

Norbert Sudhaus

Munich 1972
Marathon

Bit chunky for a marathon runner, was my first thought. And, sure enough, he wasn't a marathon runner at all. He was a German student having a laugh, a pretty effective one, at the expense of 72,000 spectators in the Olympic Stadium in Munich and poor Frank Shorter, the US marathon runner, who was following him into the stadium.

Norbert had been put up to it for a bet. In a German vest, purloined from somewhere, he joined the Olympic marathon a quarter of a mile from the finish and ran into the stadium to be heralded by the German crowd as a hero. But as he thundered around the track, very un-long-distance-runner-like, the officials grew suspicious. He barely had a bead of sweat on his brow. They twigged and he was corralled and bundled off the track, just as Shorter, the genuine leader, came into the stadium. Boos and catcalls were ringing round the arena, meant for the prankster, but assumed by the baffled American as meant for him. He must have been wondering why he was receiving the worst reception of any Olympic gold medallist possibly in the entire history of the Games.

Things didn't become much clearer to him afterwards, either. Asked about 'that guy' by the media, he just looked bemused and said, 'What guy?' But there was a happy ending. Apparently, after the race, Shorter went back to his room in the village and celebrated victory by drinking three gins in the bath. That must have been what passed for a warm-down in those days.

There are two footnotes to this story. One is that on only three occasions has an American won the marathon and each time they were not the first to enter the stadium at the finish. The first time was in 1904, one of the most bizarre and hilarious

As he thundered around the track, very un-long-distance-runner-like, the officials grew suspicious.

On only three occasions has an American won the marathon and each time they were not the first to enter the stadium at the finish.

episodes in Olympic history, but potentially fatal.

This might give you a snapshot. The competitors included a five-foot-tall Cuban who had hitchhiked to St Louis and was proposing to run in heavy street shoes, long trousers and a beret. The start of the race was delayed while a kindly discus thrower cut off the the Cuban's pants at the knees. The marathon also contained the first Africans to compete in the Olympics, two Tswana tribesmen who were in St Louis to enact battle scenes from the Boer War at the Louisiana Exposition. Among others of significance were Jack Lorz of New York and fellow countryman Thomas Hicks, who had recently finished second in the Boston Marathon.

The organisers of the race knew next to nothing about marathons. The course contained seven hills and the dusty roads were turned into a sandstorm by the cars that were allowed to plough along before, beside and behind the athletes. They were also running in temperatures of 90 degrees. Needless to say, the toll was severe.

One runner was found lying unconscious by the side of the road. One of the Africans was chased off the course and through a cornfield by two large dogs. The five-foot Cuban couldn't resist stopping to chat to spectators, and then the apples he scrumped gave him cramps.

Over three hours had gone by and still the stadium awaited the leader. Eventually, Lorz appeared and was initially hailed the winner. However, it soon transpired that, probably sensibly, he had stopped running after nine miles and hitched a lift for the next seven. He readily admitted his prank, but was slapped with a lifetime ban (overturned the following year).

The real winner was Hicks, who finished in a time of 3 hours 28 minutes 53 seconds, and probably in a drug-fuelled trance. He certainly wouldn't be declared the winner in these days of anti-chemical enhancement. So exhausted was he at the halfway stage that his team had administered an oral dose of strychnine mixed with raw egg white. At his next wobble, they upped the dose to strychnine plus brandy. Apparently, two more of these little pick-me-ups were offered before he finally – obliviously – made his way to the finish, and he was in a state of complete collapse when he crossed the line. He had lost 10 pounds in weight during the afternoon and thankfully announced his retirement when he came to. They reckon one more dose of strychnine would have killed him.

The other occasion on which an American winner came into the stadium second was London 1908. This is the famous story of Dorando Pietri and Johnny Hayes (see page 135).

As for pranks, I was in a team sport, so you'd expect us to play ridiculous jokes on one another, and we duly did. Probably the best was against me. It was captured on film as well – recorded for our BBC *Gold Fever* production before the Sydney Olympics – but for obvious reasons it had to be cut out.

We were training in Seville and staying in a hotel. I was sharing a room with Matt, as usual. For some reason, I went back to the room without him and as I passed the open bathroom door, I jumped with the shock of my life. The lights weren't working and yet I could dimly see a peculiar figure in there, mysteriously still. I tried to remember I was a 38-year-old man, father of three, who didn't believe in ghosts. On closer inspection, it was revealed to be a statue lugged up from another floor (this had James Cracknell's and Tim Foster's fingerprints all over it, literally) and dressed in my rowing gear.

I swore loudly, but needing to use the facilities, I edged round it and went to the loo anyway. It was only later that I discovered a little telltale red light on a video recorder and understood that the whole incident had been captured for posterity. We did watch it, everyone crying with laughter, but probably took the right decision not to let the world watch, too.

I was in a team sport, so you'd expect us to play ridiculous jokes on one another, and we duly did. Probably the best was against me.

Oscar Swahn
London 1908 to Antwerp 1920
Running-deer shooting

I thought I was getting on a bit when I competed in my last Olympics, but I was practically a youngster compared to this guy. Oscar Swahn of Sweden won a team silver medal in the running-deer shooting event at the Antwerp Olympics 1920 at the age of 72 years and 280 days, a record to this day, and quite unlikely to be beaten, I would say. That silver represented his fifth Olympic medal at his third Games; he was at Stockholm in 1912, in between London and Antwerp.

I also thought I knew my Olympic history, but I had no idea that athletes at the start of the last century were obliged to kill wildlife in pursuit of their medals. That's what I imagined, anyway, from the title of Mr Swahn's event. As it happens, though, no running deer were actually slaughtered. Instead, the competitors (flowing beard and greatcoat permitting) fired shots at moving deer-shaped targets, until the event was discontinued in 1956. In some ways, unless you're a vegetarian, this is rather disappointing news. I imagined a more exotic competition with large-antlered beasts running amok through the undergrowth, causing danger to the officials and havoc with the results. But no.

I also thought I knew my Olympic history, but I had no idea that athletes at the start of the last century were obliged to kill wildlife in pursuit of their medals.

Seeing this picture reminds me that, as physiological specimens, athletes have come quite a long way, although I do admit to former possession of quite a bushy beard. It was around 1983, when Ann first started to notice me. I have always maintained it was the beard that attracted her. For some reason, she denies this and accuses me of simply being too lazy to shave, adding that, if I had my way, I'd turn into an Oscar Swahn-lookalike and live on my own like a hermit.

I think the point she is making is that I am not a great one for fuss and bother. At the start of my career I went almost everywhere in slippers – carpet slippers from Marks and Spencer. They were comfortable, that's why, and very handy for slipping on and off near the river bank. It never occurred to me they were slightly uncool. It wouldn't have bothered me if it had.

I suppose they could be slightly inconvenient. I remember once doing a training run down Mount Vesuvius in Italy, which given the volcanic ash everywhere, was quite a slipping and sliding exercise. I am almost proud to report, however, that I conducted the whole run in my carpet slippers, and was forced into trainers and flip flops under sufferance as my career progressed.

At the start of my career I went almost everywhere in slippers – carpet slippers from Marks and Spencer. They were comfortable, that's why, and very handy for slipping on and off near the river bank. It never occurred to me they were slightly uncool.

Oscar and I may have more in common than I originally thought. Certainly I enjoyed my beard era. It was especially useful in winter time for extra warmth, like my own personal snood, but it tended to ice up on particularly cold days, and in the end it just became too annoying.

Oscar and I may have more in common than I originally thought. Certainly I enjoyed my beard era. It was especially useful in winter time for extra warmth, like my own personal snood, but it tended to ice up on particularly cold days, and in the end it just became too annoying. I sometimes think – thereby backing up everything Ann says about me – that were it not for the functions I have to attend, I wouldn't mind going back to a beard.

As for guns, they were not completely unknown in my family because I have it on quite good authority that one of my grandfathers used to do a little poaching to supplement the family meals. I should imagine that running deer were out of the question, but the odd rabbit here and there might have helped a working-class family to eat well.

Daley Thompson

Athens 1982
Decathlon

To me, this sums up Daley. His rivals in the decathlon have crashed out on the ground, exhausted at the end of the competition, and he stands there among them, hands on his hips, apparently nonchalant, clearly the winner. Although this picture is actually from the European Championships in 1982, it perfectly epitomises Daley's philosophy and desire, which of course made him such a great Olympian too,

Obviously, he was a great athlete. Some people, Seb Coe included, think he's the best athlete ever. My personal view is that he doesn't make the top five of great British Olympians. I'd put Seb above him, and Kelly Holmes, certainly Ben Ainslie, and, all modesty aside, myself and Matt Pinsent. Arguably, Chris Hoy and Bradley Wiggins deserve to be rated higher.

I say that because, to me, athletes compete at the decathlon if they are great all-rounders instead of being supreme in one event. Daley's forte was power. He threw well, he sprinted well, and when it came to the 1500 metres, he'd usually built such a lead that all he had to do was lumber round to emerge the victor overall. This is not to diminish his all-round ability; just an observation based on fact. He ran the 100 metres in 10.44 in Los Angeles, while Carl Lewis was winning the individual event in under 10 seconds. He threw the javelin 65.24 metres, while the Olympic champion's distance was 86.76 metres. Daley's long jump was nearly half a metre short of Lewis's, who added the long jump to his gold haul. And while Seb won the Olympic 1500 in a time of 3:33.53, Daley was winning his decathlon gold medal in the relatively pedestrian time of 4:35.00.

He was a Goliath of a guy, a two-time Olympic gold medallist, winning the decathlon at both Moscow in 1980 and LA in 1984. I always thought he was very arrogant with it.

169

He trained on Christmas Day. That was unheard of in those days. But when he explained, I immediately saw the logic. He said that he knew his opponents would take the day off.

Still, on the basis of beating everyone else in the decathlon, including the big beast, West German world record holder Jurgen Hingsen, he became an iconic British sporting legend and understandably so. He was a Goliath of a guy, a two-time Olympic gold medallist, winning the decathlon at both Moscow in 1980 and LA in 1984. I always thought he was somewhat arrogant with it, but that does not diminish his sporting ability. It just wasn't a style I can relate to. Daley talked a great deal about what he was going to do, while I've always preferred the approach that you let your sport do the talking.

Daley liked to stir things up a little. He caused controversy in LA by wearing a T-shirt on his lap of honour that read: 'Is The World's 2nd Greatest Athlete Gay?' – a direct and, some would say, invasive reference to Carl Lewis – and whistling through the national anthem. His attitude was often described as irreverent. I thought it shaved into rude.

But, having said all that, I have to thank him. That picture made a real impact on me. I was a rower, but not a great one. I had yet to make an appearance at the Olympic Games, and could have been accused of arrogance, or at least naivete, myself. So many people at Marlow Rowing Club were telling me that I would be an Olympic champion, I had begun to think it was my due. All I had to do was wait for the logical progression and one day I would be holding a gold medal.

The incident that changed all that was being eliminated in the single sculls at the 1983 senior World Championships. Never mind winning, taking a medal, or even reaching the final, I wasn't in the top 12. That shook me and gave me a well-earned dose of realism. If I wanted an example of what you had to do to reach the very top of your sport, I had that of Daley Thompson right in front of my eyes.

I remember hearing that he trained on Christmas Day. That was unheard of in those days. But when he explained, I immediately saw the logic. He said that he knew his opponents would take the day off, so that was his opportunity to gain an advantage on them. From that day onwards, I trained on Christmas Day. Admittedly, at first it was more a case of getting over my hangover from the pub crawl on Christmas Eve, but as time went on, it became a vital component of my professional attitude to rowing, as I saw it.

It wasn't that I thought it would do me physical harm to miss one day of training; it was much more a state of mind. If I missed Christmas Day, think how much easier it would be to dodge other days. That was the ideology. One day could lead to more days, and that would have been catastrophic.

Seb Coe once said, 'Daley is a Stalinist. It's not enough for him to win; he has to mentally destroy his opponent,' and I understood that concept. I remember Matt and I rowing in Vienna. It was our first World Championships together and we won. As we crossed that line, Matt wanted to collapse over his oars after the stupendous exertion. God knows, I wanted to as well, but I barked, 'Sit UP!' because I wanted all our beaten rivals to think that we still had more in hand. I wanted them to think that we were invincible and they were just rowing for the minor places.

I thought that for years. It was only much later, perhaps even after retirement, that I realised it wasn't the opponents I was trying to convince. It was me. We weren't conditioning the opposition. I wanted – *needed* – to convince myself we were invincible. We were conditioning ourselves.

That's why I will always remember this picture. Daley was partly sending a message to his opponents, but mainly he was sending one to himself. Years later someone asked him why he was still standing when everyone else had collapsed. He said, 'I would have loved to, but there wasn't any room on the floor for me.'

As we crossed that line, Matt wanted to collapse over his oars after the stupendous exertion. God knows, I wanted to as well, but I barked, 'Sit UP!' because I wanted all our beaten rivals to think that we still had more in hand.

Natalie du Toit

Beijing 2008

10 kilometre open water swim

Natalia Partyka

Beijing 2008

Table tennis

These are athletes. I state the obvious because, of course, they are visibly unusual athletes. But not because they lack the mental strength, the physical prowess and the huge determination that separates the merely talented from champions. In some ways, talent is the least of it. It is what you do next that matters.

Natalie du Toit was already a junior swimming champion in South Africa when she was knocked off her scooter by a car after a training session, and subsequently had to have her left leg amputated at the knee. She was back in the swimming pool before she learned to walk again.

'Swimming is my passion,' she has said. 'Going out there in the water, it feels as if there's nothing wrong with me. I don't think one leg, two legs. You try your best. That's what counts.'

Du Toit and Natalia Partyka, the Polish table tennis player, made history at Beijing in 2008 by competing in both the Olympics and Paralympics. Both had qualified in the able-bodied version of their events, which, given the tiny percentage of human beings who ever make it to any Olympics, makes the word 'disabled' seem wildly out of place.

In the Olympic event, du Toit, with half the leg-propulsion potential of her rivals, finished 16th in the 10 kilometre open swim, just 1 minute 22.2 seconds behind the gold medallist. Partyka didn't make it to an Olympic final, but perhaps just being there was a life-changing, culture-busting moment all of

'Swimming is my passion. Going out there in the water, it feels as if there's nothing wrong with me. I don't think one leg, two legs. You try your best. That's what counts.'
Natalie du Toit

173

Just being there was a life-changing, culture-busting moment all of its own, especially in a country such as China.

its own, especially in a country such as China, which had a reputation of preferring to keep its disabled citizens out of sight. Both Natalie and Natalia cleaned up in the Paras.

Some people thought it was the first time such a crossover had ever happened, but that's just because news travels faster these days. There are actually quite a few instances of astonishing athletes who refused to recognise so-called disability as anything but a spur to training harder.

Looking back through the record books, there was a New Zealand archer who crossed the Olympic/Paralympic divide, a US runner and a famous Italian archer, Paola Fantato, who competed at five successive Paralympics between 1988 and 2004. But it's not even a recent phenomenon. US gymnast George Eyser won three golds, two silvers and a bronze in the 1904 St Louis Olympics, long before the Paralympics was thought of, despite having a wooden leg, which he had acquired after he was run over by a train.

Oliver Halassy was a Hungarian amputee, also the victim of a train accident, who won two golds and silver in the water polo, competing in 1928, 1932 and 1936. The tragic footnote to his story – perhaps an extreme case of politics interfering in sport – is that he was apparently murdered in 1946 by a Soviet soldier, when walking down a street in Budapest.

Another Hungarian, Karoly Takacs, took part in the pistol shooting event at the 1948 London Olympics, despite his right hand having been shattered by a grenade 10 years earlier. Undaunted, he taught himself to shoot with his left hand instead.

These stories are always so powerful, the inspiration they provide so fantastic, that I find it hard to hold to my innate belief that ultimately sport is about the strongest, fastest, furthest. Sport is about measuring the best on the day. In that moment, it is unarguable. You win or you lose. As I've said many times, ideally I'd like sport to be without any demarcation lines at all. Throw them all in there, no categories, and let the best man or woman emerge triumphant.

With that in mind, I have seen the Paralympics as, I suppose, a sporting consolation prize. But I have been taught there is a bigger picture. Sometimes the playing field simply isn't level. People have accidents, they have disabilities, and yet they still want to challenge themselves to be the best they can be on the sports field. Why shouldn't they? And perhaps, when they win, they have an even greater prize than a gold medal. They know they've shifted the attitudes of some old sporting die-hards, including me.

> *These stories are always so powerful, the inspiration they provide so fantastic, that I find it hard to hold to my innate belief that ultimately sport is about the strongest, fastest, furthest.*

US Basketball Team
Munich 1972
Basketball final

They had won every single match they had played in Olympic history, the US basketball team. From 1936, when they beat Estonia 52–28, to the semi-finals of the competition in 1972, the record was 62 wins, 0 losses.

Interestingly, their rivals in the final were the Soviet Union, a mirror image of the political world. The Cold War ensured that the Soviets and Americans often lined up on the opposite side of any argument. And this turned out to be an argument. In American sporting history, certainly, it is known as the most controversial of all time.

The ins-and-outs of basketball rules are unknown territory for me, but what is dramatically clear is that the Soviets were leading by a point with six seconds left to play. Then Doug Collins of Indiana State University was fouled and scored with his two free throws. That made the score 50–49 to the States. Cue huge American celebrations, because with no time to go they thought they'd won. But a confusing argument was put forward by the Soviets. They had apparently called a 'time-out',

That made the score 50–49 to the States. Cue huge American celebrations, because with no time to go they thought they'd won.

A 6ft 7in Soviet youngster, Sacha Belov, scored the winning basket. Cue huge Soviet celebrations.

and after consultation with the British chief of the International Amateur Basketball Federation, Mr R. William Jones (whose business it wasn't, but he became involved anyway), it was decided that the game should continue with three seconds on the clock.

At that point a 6ft 7in Soviet youngster, Sacha Belov, scored the winning basket. Cue huge Soviet celebrations and the devastated US reaction captured in this picture.

Even then it wasn't over. The United States filed a protest, which was heard by a five-man jury of appeal. Five men, five countries – Poland, Hungary, Cuba, Puerto Rico and Italy. Funnily enough, they voted in favour, by three to two, of the Soviet basketball team. For the US team coach, Hank Iba, it was a horrendous day made marginally worse by having his pocket picked of $370 while signing the official protest.

I know from, thankfully rare, personal experience that red-hot favourites can lose. In my case, it was at Henley Royal Regatta in 1986. Already an Olympic gold medallist, I was in the final of the diamond sculls, up against a lightweight from Denmark. Impeded by either arrogance or ignorance, I was about to learn an important lesson.

I didn't really take much interest in the guy I was rowing against. I knew who he was – Bjarne Eltang, the reigning world champion – but I didn't know anything about him tactically. I was concentrating on myself and my tactics. In a side-by-side race, which this was, it was a case of pushing past him, building a lead, watching him get demoralized and me getting to the finish line first.

After 30 seconds I led by a length. 'God, this is all right,' I'm thinking, surprised to be so far ahead so soon. After two minutes I was three lengths in front. 'This is more than all right. This is fantastic,' I'm thinking now. Then I notice he is beginning to close the gap and I've left most of my energy behind, building that early lead in my excitement. He caught me up, rowed past me and left me at a virtual standstill. A *lightweight*. It was devastating. In trying to kill him off, I killed myself instead.

Afterwards, the Olympic sculler, Chris Baillieu, came up to me and said, 'The thing about Eltang is that he's not a very fast starter but he never gives up.' I thought, 'Why didn't someone tell me that beforehand.' But it was my fault. It's single sculling, you and a boat. You have no one to blame but yourself. Maybe that's why I preferred rowing in a team.

Years later, perspective did come to at least one member of that US basketball team. In 1992, Kenny Davis said: 'I went back to my room and cried alone that night. But every time I get to feeling sorry for myself, I think of the Israeli kids who were killed at those Games … Think of being in a helicopter with your hands tied behind your back and a hand grenade rolling towards you … and compare that to not getting a gold medal. If that final game is the worst injustice that ever happens to the guys on that team, we'll all come out of this life pretty good.'

'Think of being in a helicopter with your hands tied behind your back and a hand grenade rolling towards you … and compare that to not getting a gold medal. If that final game is the worst injustice that ever happens to the guys on that team, we'll all come out of this life pretty good.'
Kenny Davis

179

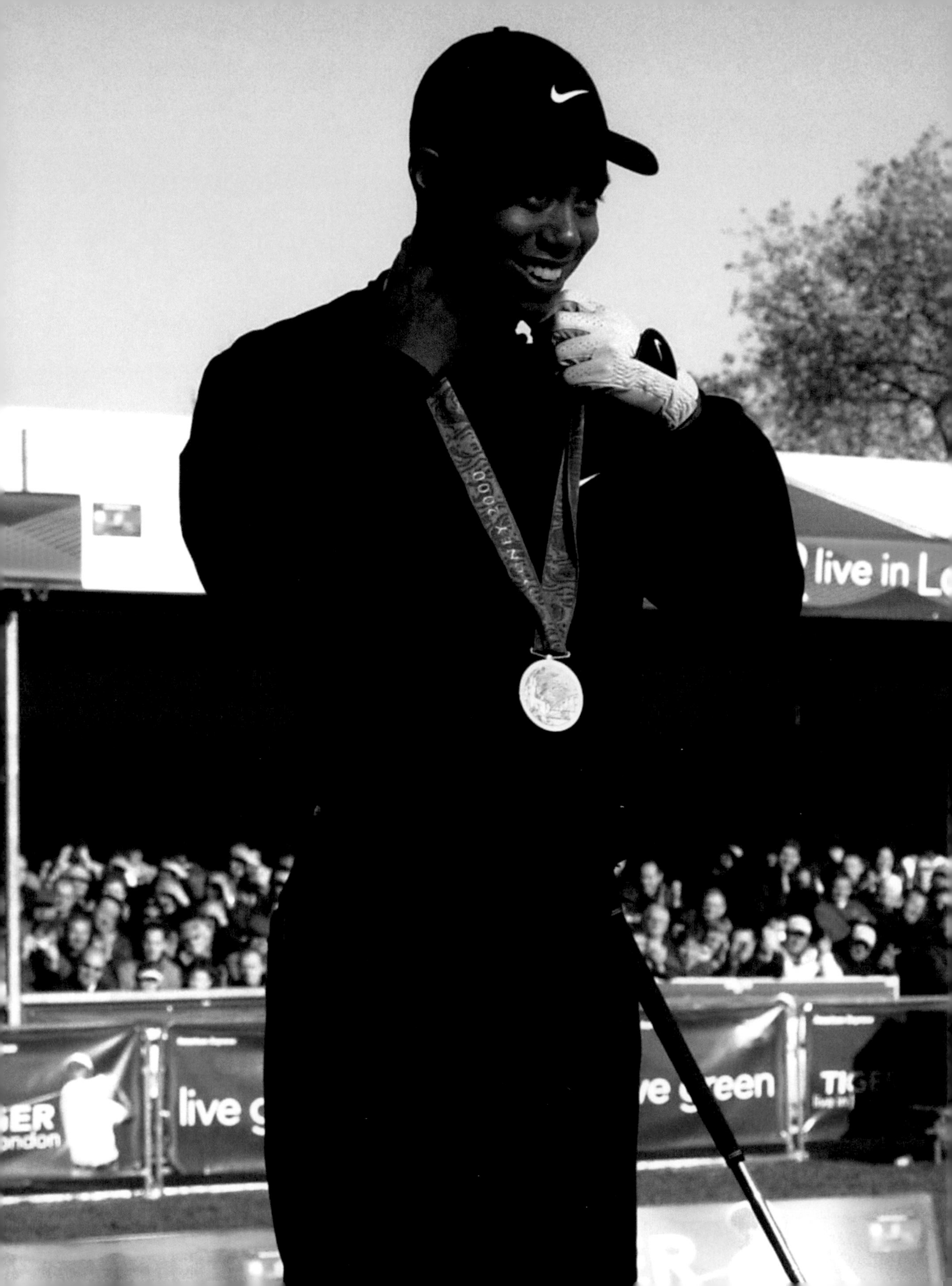
live in Lo
live g
ve green
TIG

Tiger Woods
Hyde Park 2000

You could be looking into the future here. Tiger Woods could receive an Olympic gold medal of his own in 2016 when golf is reintroduced to the Summer Olympic schedule after a break of over a century. On this occasion, though, the medal was not his own but belonged to a friend of mine, Matt Pinsent.

It was shortly after the Sydney Olympics. I had officially retired and here was a perk. Time to slip off and learn a thing or two about a sport that has frustrated me for years. I love golf and sometimes hate it. It really annoys me that ball-playing athletes – footballers and tennis players, for instance – can almost instantly become single-figure handicappers at golf. I, on the other hand, seem to have played off 14 for the last 30 years.

So it was with some interest that Matt and I attended a Tiger Woods golf clinic in Hyde Park, just to see if we could pick up a few pointers to hone our game. The event was called 'Tiger in the Park' and we were invited to watch the master at work, designated VIPs and sitting a couple of rows back in the audience.

This was a scary proximity. All Matt and I could do was pray he didn't invite us up to hit a few balls towards a hole that had been lodged into the grass a hundred or so yards away. As always happens when you're thinking, 'Oh God, I hope he doesn't pull us out of the crowd,' we were pulled out of the crowd. I was eyeing a bucket of balls and imagining just how much damage I could do to the audience if he let me loose

As more and more women admitted to affairs with the world's greatest living sportsman, I had one stunned reaction. 'How did he find the time?'

on the tee, but then Matt came up with a brilliant idea. He hung his gold medal round Tiger's neck, and despite all the glittering prizes in golf that had already gone Tiger's way, you could see he was really blown away by it. Suitably distracted, he didn't ask us to hit any balls and we were able to reclaim our seats without any lawsuits pending for accidental GBH.

But I don't really consider that I've *met* Tiger. On that occasion it was significant that we were separated from the general public in the VIP marquee, but Tiger was separated from the VIPs somewhere else. Now that is real fame. He is right up there, I would say, along with Muhammad Ali, as the most famous sportsman on the planet. And that was before his extra-curricular love-life came to light.

When the news slowly emerged that more and more women admitted to affairs with the world's greatest living sportsman, I had one stunned reaction. 'How did he find the time?' It seemed incredible to me that someone as obviously devoted to his sport, to training, to practice, to fitness, would actually have enough hours in the day to meet cocktail waitresses.

Well, I and everybody else was wrong. He managed it and I suspect the result – not of the scandal, which is nobody's real business except his ex-wife's – is a diminished sportsman. Not hugely diminished and not necessarily forever, but in some ways I feel his aura as a golfer has been broken. There is a vulnerability about him now; or, to put it another way, his opponents sense a vulnerability about him now. It is like blood to a shark. Where once he would have broken their spirit just by turning up, now he has given them the strength and motivation to challenge him. Sport is a ruthless business. Even fame can't protect you from that.

Tiger's fame is of a different order from anything I've ever known. His separation from us that day in the park was a graphic example of that. To be that well-known, discussed, dissected, is not something I have ever wanted. Even speaking in public was a torment to me to begin with. I realised exactly

To be that well-known, discussed, dissected, is not something I have ever wanted. Even speaking in public was a torment to me to begin with.

how much of a torment after the LA Olympics, when the town of Marlow decided to put on an open-topped bus for those of us from the local rowing club who came back with medals. To be honest, most of the onlookers were shoppers, mildly baffled about who we could be. When the bus came to a halt, we piled off to be greeted by the local mayor, who was going to present me with a gift. What could be daunting about that? But I froze. Completely froze. I was petrified he was going to ask me to say a few words and I knew that I wouldn't be able to say a thing. Luckily, the mayor went on talking and the moment passed. I wasn't a kid, either. I was 22, but having been shy all my life, the transition wasn't going to be easy. Eventually, I did manage to open my jaw and get out a few words of thanks – my parents had always insisted on politeness – but it was my idea of purgatory.

I'm fine now. I can give speeches and presentations three nights a week and suffer no nerves at all. But, even so, I have nothing like the level of fame under which Tiger Woods is obliged to operate. So I wish him well. He's still a bloody good golfer. If I had his touch round the green, I wouldn't *still* be playing off 14.

Emil Zatopek

Helsinki 1952
Triple long-distance champion
Marathon

He ran as though he was in agony. Arms flailing, head rolling, an expression of terrible pain on his face, but as he explained with typical modesty, 'I wasn't talented enough to run and smile at the same time.' In fact, he was a mild-mannered Hercules, one of the most gracious, sporting, unassuming Olympic athletes who ever lived.

There is something very special that appeals to me about the story of Emil Zatopek, son of a Czech carpenter, who enjoyed running so much as a child that he used to race his mother's grey Chinese geese, which she was intending to fatten for the pot. She was pretty angry about that. Instead of nurturing the birds, he was coaching them to a state of lean and unappetizing athleticism.

He never thought of himself as hugely talented – perhaps he wasn't – but he trained literally night and day to overcome deficiencies in his running. He used to do interval training in the hours of darkness, so intent was he on not wasting time. The end result was one of the most astonishing athletic Olympic performances of all time. That is surely unarguable.

He never thought of himself as hugely talented – perhaps he wasn't – but he trained literally night and day to overcome deficiencies in his running.

He had begun his adult life working in a shoe factory in Zlin. By sheer hard, painstaking work, the boy who loved racing geese graduated into the man who would become the greatest long-distance runner of his era.

In London in 1948, he had won gold and silver medals, but Helsinki was to be his bravura performance. His preparations had been hampered by a virus, which turned into a serious illness. Doctors warned him not to compete in Helsinki at all, concerned that he could do permanent damage to his heart. He took no notice whatsoever. He decided to cure himself with a homemade brew of tea and lemons, and succeeded in doing just that.

What happened next I still find hard to believe. He was world record holder and reigning champion in the 10,000 metres, so perhaps it is reasonable that he dominated the race from the seventh lap, with his relentlessly even pace, beating his nearest rival to the finish line by 15 seconds.

But in the 5000 metres he faced serious contenders in the shape of the favourite from Germany, Herbert Schade, Alain Mimoun of France and the two Brits, Gordon Pirie and Chris Chataway. Schade decided to run from the front to try to disrupt Zatopek's rock-steady rhythm. In this he was entirely unsuccessful. After 2000 metres, the Czech came alongside him and said amiably, 'Herbert, do a couple of laps with me.' Not surprisingly, the German ignored him, gritting his teeth in the guts of the race. In some, the chatty gesture would have been pure gamesmanship. In Zatopek, it was unaffected sporting generosity. He eased into the lead but, on the back straight before the finish, three of his rivals sped past him. He thought he had lost. But the greatest champions call on reserves of energy simply unavailable to the rest of humanity. He ran wide on the final bend and won by two yards at the finish line. He was now a double Olympic gold medallist at these Games. That would be enough for most people.

Instead, he decided to run the Olympic marathon – an event

Instead, he decided to run the Olympic marathon – an event he had never run before in his life.

He does remain, however, one of my favourite athletes of all time; probably because he proves my point. There isn't, and never will be, a substitute for hard work.

he had never run before in his life. No one has to tell me how hard that race can be, and clearly no professional athlete on earth would contemplate tackling these three events at any Olympics these days.

Inexperienced as he was, Zatopek decided to shadow the favourite for the race, Jim Peters of Great Britain. How must Peters have enjoyed that! And the pleasure was made even more dubious for the British man at the halfway stage, when Zatopek casually inquired whether the pace was fast enough. More gritted teeth. 'No, too slow,' Peters managed to gasp, fighting with his own exhaustion, and hoping he would provoke the Czech into a burst of speed that would ultimately knock him out of the race.

Instead, Peters retired at the 20 mile mark with cramp and Zatopek, seeing off all the other competitors, ran the last five miles on his own, chatting to the crowd and the policemen as he passed. He arrived in the stadium to a tumultuous ovation, richly deserved.

It is quite possible that he could have won Olympic gold again in Melbourne four years later, but training with his wife on his shoulders had been one ambition too far. He developed a hernia and although he raced, he did not make the final reckoning. He does remain, however, one of my favourite athletes of all time; probably because he proves my point. There isn't, and never will be, a substitute for hard work.

Picture credits

We would like to thank the following for kindly supplying images for this book:

Getty Images – Ben Ainsley, Bob Beamon, Fanny Blankers-Koen, Chris Boardman, Steve Bradbury, Cassius Clay, Seb Coe, Mary Decker, Eric the Eel, Birgit Fischer, Cathy Freeman, Florence Griffith Joyner, Eric Heiden, Walter Herrmann, Kelly Holmes, Israeli Hostage Crisis, Knud Enemark Jensen, Ben Johnson, Michael Johnson, Eric Liddell, Vanderlei de Lima, Greg Louganis, Olympic Stadium 1896, Spyridon Louis, Edwin Moses, Opening Ceremony 1984, Harold Osborn, Dick Fosbury, Jesse Owens, Dorando Pietri, Paula Radcliffe, Steve Redgrave, Tommie Smith, John Carlos and Peter Norman, Mark Spitz, Ingemar Stenmark, Norbert Sudhaus, Oscar Swahn, Daley Thompson, Natalie du Toit, Natalia Partyka, US Basketball Team and Emil Zatopek.

Paul Vathis/Press Association Images – Nadia Comaneci.

Anthony Harvey/PA Archive/Press Association Images – Tiger Woods.

David Faulkner – GB Men's Hockey Team.

akg-images/Ullstein bild – Aladar Gerevich.

John H. Shore – Steve Redgrave, Diamond single sculls, Henley.

Reuters/Russell Boyce – With Ann and the children, Sydney 2000.

Acknowledgements

Special thanks to Sue Mott, who has helped bring to life both the unique moments of Olympic history and my recollection and reflections of them. I couldn't have done it without you Sue.

Thanks also to my PA Melanie Clift, and to Michael Pask, Sarah Wooldridge and Katie Robinson at IMG for their continued encouragement and support.

Warm thanks to all at Headline Publishing for helping make this book a reality.

And finally, deepest thanks to my family, Ann, Natalie, Sophie and Zak for their endless love and support throughout my Olympic journey and beyond.